MEMOIRS OF LI HUNG CHANG

W & D Downey, Copyright

Li Hung Chang
With Lord Salisbury and Lord Curzon.

MEMOIRS OF
LI HUNG CHANG

EDITED BY

WILLIAM FRANCIS MANNIX

WITH AN INTRODUCTION BY

HON. JOHN W. FOSTER

BOSTON AND NEW YORK

HOUGHTON MIFFLIN COMPANY

The Riverside Press Cambridge

1913

EDITOR'S PREFACE

It is believed that the memoirs of Li Hung Chang will speak for themselves, or, better, for the famous Viceroy, who in the flesh was ever ready to speak for the betterment of his country and her people. Still it is deemed advisable here to call the reader's attention to the form in which the translated transcriptions are given to the public.

The Viceroy was by no means a careful diarist; indeed, the contrary was true. Many of his manuscripts were left in Hankow when he went north to Tientsin; and the writings of twenty-four years in the latter city were undisturbed in his rich private lodge until about two years ago, when from half a score of cities of China — Hankow, Canton, Shanghai, Nanking, Suchau, Peking, Tientsin, and others — his writings were collected by a provincial governor of the two Kwangs provinces, a nephew of Li's, and deposited in the palatial residence of the former Viceroy at Canton.

With the permission of the Imperial Government nearly two years ago, and the consent of the trustees and heirs of Li Hung Chang's estate, the great mass of documents and notes were examined, and carefully translated by Major R. Emmet Roberts, a secretary of the late Viceroy, assisted by Drs. Wang, of Peking, and Hsiu-Tsai, the Elder, of Canton.

Over one hundred and seventy thousand words of the Viceroy's memoirs were translated and diligently compared; and from this large mass, these notes — comprising the only writings of the Grand Secretary that have ever been rendered into English — are for the first time offered to the public of England and America.

It will be remarked that various subjects are treated under separate titles. The original manuscripts, found in many different cities of China, and placed at our disposal through the great kindness of family and friends, and with the consent of the Imperial Government, — nearly two years ago, — treated, of course, of a multitude of subjects. A line — a column of characters — would be the sum-total of comment at a particular time; while, later on, when perhaps the Viceroy occupied a wholly different post, maybe in another part of the empire, he would revert to the subject and, it might be, write three, five, or twenty pages. Still later, again, he would express himself upon the same subject from a different or new viewpoint.

It was thought best, therefore, — and particularly as it was manifestly out of the question, because of their great bulk, to publish his entire writings, which amount to the equivalent of some one million six hundred thousand English words, — to make selections from his diary and other manuscripts to be grouped together under appropriate heads, at the same time arranging them chronologically.

And this calls for the second and final explanation. While the translators found little difficulty in rendering into English the beautifully executed characters of the great Viceroy, they were sorely distracted in the matter of determining dates; for in his earlier years, and up to the time of his appearance as Viceroy at Tientsin, Li marked his manuscripts in a way of his own: in strange cycles and reigns. So confusing was this, even to the Chinese scholars engaged in the work, that they agreed to omit many of them, unanimously asserting that to ascertain with exactness when each entry was made would require a year's time of an expert Chinese historian!

Even from 1870 onward, Li, though making use generally of more modern methods, went to extremes in the dating of some of his entries and manuscripts, writing, for example, "12th Day of the 5th Moon, of the 10th Year of Kuang Su. Hour of the Sheep," to identify the time of putting upon paper a few unimportant statements, and quite ignoring to state time or place in connection with comments or historical data of world-wide interest. In some of these latter, dates have been supplied, for the purpose of associating the matter with the proper period of the Viceroy's life, rather than because of any belief that either their presence or absence would add to or detract from the political or literary value of his words.

It may be said that this volume does not presume to present all that Li Hung Chang wrote upon the subjects given herein under the various part titles, or even a larger portion; but in the making of the selections it has been the aim of the Editor to include those which he believed held the widest and most enduring interest.

W. F. M.

SHANGHAI, December 1, 1912.

CONTENTS

INTRODUCTION

LI HUNG CHANG was not only the greatest man the Chinese race has produced in modern times, but, in a combination of qualities, the most unique personality of the past century among all the nations of the world. He was distinguished as a man of letters; as a soldier in important campaigns he rendered valuable services to his country; as a statesman for thirty years he maintained a recognised preëminence over his countrymen in the oldest and most populous nation of the earth; and as a diplomat his achievements entitle him to a front rank in the international relations of all history.

The last one hundred years have produced many men of scholarship, several great generals, a number of statesmen of distinguished ability and success, and a few diplomats of high rank; but no one of these can be singled out as having combined in his person all these attainments in such an eminent degree as Li Hung Chang. Because of his distinction in all these fields of human activity, we should welcome these memoirs, extracted from his voluminous diary, as a valuable contribution for the better understanding of his character and services.

In forming an estimate of any man, the age in which he lived and his environment are to be considered. It is hardly just to estimate the character and attainments of Li Hung Chang according to the standard of European or Western nations. His education was exclusively Oriental, and until he had passed the allotted Scriptural period of man's life, his had been spent entirely in China. His knowledge of our civilisation was only such as could be acquired in the motley society of a treaty port. As a statesman he had to deal with a very conservative and bigoted constituency, and with associates prejudiced against and ignorant of foreign nations. He was born and reared in a rural community, of worthy but not distinguished parentage. His father, of the "gentry" class, had successfully passed the examinations, but held no official position, and was possessed of no means of procuring his son's advancement beyond affording him an opportunity to pursue his studies and fit himself for the examinations. These he successfully passed in all grades, and in the final contest at Peking he came out with distinguished honours among twenty thousand competitors. Later he was made a member of the Han-lin College, which corresponds somewhat to the French Academy.

He therefore had reason to take pride in his accomplishments and standing as a scholar, and throughout his career he was recognised by his countrymen as in the first rank among the men of letters. Some of his writings in prose and poetry had wide circulation in the empire and gained him much praise. His diary shows that he himself put great store on his literary attainments, and until late in life, when absorbed in the weighty affairs of state, his highest ambition was to be recognised as the poet-laureate of his people.

In his early manhood he thought only of a literary career; but the course of public affairs was destined to defeat his expectation, and turn his life into an entirely different channel. The Taiping Rebellion, one of the most sanguinary in the history of the human race, had its inception during his student days; and about the time of his return from the imperial capital to his home to receive the honours which every Chinese community showers upon its successful students, the rebellion had assumed its most alarming proportions. As he reached his father's house he saw the rebels pass by on their triumphant march towards Peking. His patriotism was stirred within him as he saw the dynasty which had conferred on him such high honours and the ancient government in imminent peril. He at once set to work to raise a volunteer regiment to fall upon and harass the rear of the enemy. His diary reveals the man: "Everybody knows that a soldier is despised, and that, according to the Old Rules, I am leaving the greatest of the professions for the worst of occupations. . . . But is this a time for writing poetry? Who cares for romances when fire and sword are in the land?"

The next four years found him actively engaged in warfare; and he showed such aptitude for the profession that he had the distinction of being in command of the army which gave the death-blow to the rebellion. In this period he had under his command the American soldier, General Ward, who organised the "Ever Victorious Army," and General Gordon, who assumed its leadership on the heroic death of Ward. The diary gives great credit to the latter, and reveals not only a high appreciation of the services of Gordon, but an accurate comprehension of his merits and defects.

His military career continued for some years, owing to the disordered state of the country, coupled with civil duties of high responsibility, until he was called by the Emperor to face the crisis occasioned by the riots in Tientsin in 1870, which threatened a war with France. He brought with him to this important viceroyalty a high reputation for military skill, great administrative capacity, and devoted loyalty to the reigning dynasty; and was thenceforth regarded as one of the most famous men of his nation. His successful termination of the questions growing out of the riots so impressed the Imperial Government that it showered upon him new and almost unprecedented honours. In addition to his appointment as Viceroy of the metropolitan province of Chihli, he was named Imperial Tutor, Grand Secretary of State, Superintendent of Trade, and a noble of the first rank. These high titles made him the first official and statesman of the Government of the Emperor.

For twenty-five years continuously he discharged
the duties of these high offices from his residence at
Tientsin, with occasional visits to Peking. Because
of his high rank and of his location at the seaport
to the capital, he was brought into contact with all
persons having business with the Government, and
stood as a sentinel on the outpost for his secluded
Emperor. As the virtual head of the Chinese Foreign Office, he proved himself a match for the most
astute of the trained European diplomatists. While
the jealous guardian of his country's interests, he
always secured the confidence and esteem of the
foreign ministers with whom he conducted negotiations.

Probably no man of his time received such signal
marks of respect from his diplomatic antagonists
as he. In a serious controversy with Great Britain,
he was so straightforward and just in meeting the
demands of that Government that Sir Thomas Wade
stated that he was led to make an important concession expressly to him "in recognition of the
frankness with which he had negotiated this troublesome business." In the adjustment of the French
conflict with China of 1885, the French Minister
inserted in the treaty a renunciation of all claim for
indemnity, in order thereby "to pay a mark of
regard to the patriotic wisdom of His Excellency Li
Hung Chang."

When the Japanese Government in 1895 refused
to receive the first peace commissioners, the Prime

Minister, Count Ito, sent a message to Peking that if Li Hung Chang should be appointed, he would be received and treated with the highest consideration; and the sequel realised to the greatest extent this high estimate of his character and ability. In preparation for the ceremonies of the coronation of Emperor Nicholas II, the Czar himself sent a personal request to the Chinese Emperor that Li Hung Chang should be entrusted with the mission of special Ambassador for that occasion. It has been charged that the Viceroy was under the undue influence of Russia, it even being asserted that he had been controlled in his conduct by corrupt motives. The publication of this diary will set at rest all such insinuations, as it makes it clear that he correctly estimated the schemes of that Government, and that in his relations with it his conduct was patriotic.

In a country where office was greatly sought after as a stepping-stone to power and self-aggrandisement, it was natural that a man in his high position would have enemies among his own countrymen. His diary shows that they were numerous, and that he visited some of them with intense antagonism. But the mass of his countrymen recognised him as the first and ablest of the public officials, and paid him honour as such. This was demonstrated in a notable manner on the observance of his seventieth birthday. The Emperor sent various rich and appropriate gifts, with flattering inscriptions written in his own hand; the Empress Dowager vied with her imperial ward in her gifts; subjects of high and low degree and foreign residents lavished upon him presents and mementoes; processions, ceremonies, and banquets in Chinese profusion were the order of the day; and all culminated in an address signed by the leading officials throughout the empire, written by Chang Chi-tung, next to the Viceroy the most honoured and influential man in the country, and often his political opponent. As a specimen of Chinese eulogy an extract may be interesting: —

"You are altogether to be admired; in literature deep, in warcraft terrible, in perception acute, in genius sublime, entrenched on every side, unassailable. . . . As I stand beside you in the Han-lin, I feel how small I am, how little able to grapple with the great matters met within my province on the great river. In you we have perfect confidence, and I earnestly desire to learn from you. Compared with you, I am as a simple peasant to a picked archer, a poor jade to a fleet racer. You are men's ideal; you, like Kang Hou, enjoy the confidence of our Sovereign; yours is the glory of Chang the Councillor. You are the cynosure of all eyes."

Although in his public life the Viceroy was of stern and unrelenting character and apparently indifferent to human life, the diary reveals in many places a tender heart and sympathetic nature. His devotion to his mother was most touching. Her last illness and death occurred in a distant province while he was immersed in important affairs of state at Tientsin. He memorialised the Empress Regents for a leave of absence to go to her bedside in which he said: "She is eighty-three years old and her constitution is breaking up; and the thought of her absent son continually recurs to her and makes her illness more dangerous. When memorialist heard this his heart burned with anxiety, and his sleep and his food were worthless. Since he bade her farewell thirteen years ago, he has never seen his mother's face."

A leave of absence for one month was granted him, but before he could start on his journey news came of her death, and he petitioned for the usual retirement of three years for mourning, but the Empress Regents answered that the state of public affairs would only allow of one hundred days. But this did not satisfy his grief at the failure to reach his mother before her death, and he sent another lengthy memorial, saying: "Remorse will haunt memorialist all his life, and there is a wound in his heart that prevents him privately from enjoying a moment's respite from pain, and publicly from being of any service to the state. . . . Even if he, separated beyond hope from meeting his mother, the living from the dead, were to spend three years in lamentations at her tomb, it would not avail to relieve his soul from the poignant and inexpressible regret he feels for his lack of filial duty." We find that years after, when absorbed in his official duties, he records that fourteen years had passed that day since his mother died and that he secluded himself from all callers. "With all the incidents of my life, its trials and lamentations, its moments of joy and pride, with all and every affair of life, I cannot forget my celestial mother and all she was and is to me."

The unique correspondence with the Empress Regents brings out one of the most distinguished traits of Chinese character — veneration for parents, which has become sanctified into religious worship, and also has exercised a marked influence on the political relations of the people, the Emperor being the parental head of the nation. If the fifth commandment of the Mosaic code were as faithfully observed by Christian nations as the central doctrine of the Confucian philosophy is practised by the Celestials, the social order of the Western world would be greatly improved.

We see something more of the Viceroy's humanity when, in the midst of the battle, the grim warrior stood beside the bedside of the American General Ward, and the tears flowed down his cheeks as he thought of the soldier dying for China, "so far from his family and friends." His sympathetic nature was shown, also, in the fearful famine which during his viceroyalty visited Chihli and the neighbouring provinces. He was the most prominent agent in staying the ravages of this fatal scourge, and his energy, business capacity, and large-hearted charity were conspicuously displayed in the measures for relief. In addition to the public and charitable funds which he disbursed, the diary shows that he fed daily from his own table between one and two thousand of the starving, and from his own purse near five thousand in the near-by villages. "My mother is blessing me every day for this work; and she says the Gods as well as the people will not forget that my wealth, such as I have, is not withheld from the poor and needy."

In nothing is the diary more useful than in showing the development of Li Hung Chang's mind respecting foreigners and the Christian missionaries, and how with growing experience his ideas underwent a complete change. Early in his public career, when his knowledge was limited to a brief intercourse with foreigners at Shanghai during the Taiping Rebellion, he partook strongly of the hatred and prejudice of the masses. At this time he records, "I hate all foreigners." But fifteen years later, when he had become better acquainted with the ills which afflicted his country, and just as he was starting to assume his duties at Tientsin and put an end to the anti-foreign riots, he writes: "In spite of all dislikes, if we truly have the best interests of China at heart, we will no longer oppose the coming of the foreigner, for he is bound to come anyway, even if he must ride behind a bayonet or sit upon the big gun of a warship." And he expressed great pleasure that the Throne had selected him for the task at Tientsin. About this time he records that he is preparing an article advocating the right of foreigners to reside in China, which he intends to submit to the Throne and have printed and circulated in every province. After his coming to Tientsin foreigners were fully protected in the provinces under his administration. He was not blind to their encroachments and arrogance, but he recognised their usefulness to the country and that they were entitled to protection. At the beginning of the Boxer outbreak, when Viceroy at Canton, he reports that some of the viceroys had received orders to be prepared to despatch all foreigners, which he terms "dastardly commands. How well the authors knew better than to send such outrageous documents to me." When we call to mind the experience China has had with certain Western nations, it does not seem strange that his attachment to foreigners in general should not have been very ardent, but he came to feel the need of foreign aid, and solicited it and gave it proper welcome.

The Viceroy's mind underwent much the same experience respecting Christianity and missionaries. As he reached manhood he possessed the same ignorance and hatred of missionaries and their work as prevailed generally throughout the country, referred to them as "foreign devils," and treated their doctrines with scorn. But gradually, as he became personally better informed as to their work, he revised his judgment. Soon after assuming charge at Tientsin he notes a conference with Tseng-Kofan, the great statesman of that day, who, he says, "like myself, has changed his views exceedingly in the past five or six years, and is no longer a hater of the Christians." Fifteen years later he went so far as to put Christ and Confucius on the same exalted plane and to assert that if he were in England or America he would want to call himself a Christian. He treats their doctrines as philosophic or moral, and fails to comprehend the spiritual quality of the teaching and mission of Christ. But his prejudice against Christianity had disappeared, and he said that there were millions in China who would be benefited by a knowledge of Jesus, as they do not trouble themselves to follow Confucius. Nevertheless, the inconsistencies of the Christian nations did not fail to attract his attention. He notes how they fight among themselves and cherish most bitter hatred against each other. "The French hate the Germans, and the Russians kill the Jews, but they are all Christians when they come to China"; and he refers to the action of Great Britain in forcing opium on the Chinese as one of the impediments to the progress of Christianity, with this closing comment: "A great nation, a Christian nation above all things, has given this awful blight to the Middle Kingdom. What are our people to think?"

In the seventy-fifth year of his age, Li Hung Chang made his first journey to foreign lands. It was a memorable event in his life. The occasion of it was the coronation of the Emperor of Russia. This ceremony brought together at the ancient Muscovite capital such a representation of the nations of the earth as was never before assembled in the world. And it is safe to say that the most notable personage in that august assemblage was the representative of the "Son of Heaven," the Emperor of China. In length of public service, in the character and importance of that service and of the myriads of people in whose behalf it was rendered, in his intellectual attainments, his unique characteristics, and in his commanding personality, the Chinese representative was the most conspicuous witness of the young Czar's coronation.

Aside from his distinguished services and his high offices, he was a man well suited to be placed at the head of an imposing embassy, and to represent his imperial master. He was of pure Chinese extraction, having no mixture of Manchu blood. Although in his seventy-fifth year, he was in fair degree of health and vigour, of fine physique, full six feet in height, of commanding presence, erect and stoutly built, with dark, piercing eyes, and a face strongly moulded and indicative of strength of character, and that would command attention in any foreign circle. Dressed in his parti-coloured silken robes, and his hat decorated with the three-eyed peacock feathers, he could not fail to attract attention.

The Viceroy having made the journey to Russia via the Suez Canal, he continued the circumnavigation of the globe by way of the Western nations of

Europe and America, in the course of which he met the crowned heads and leading statesmen of those countries, received marked ovations everywhere by the officials and people, witnessed military and naval reviews, and saw the marvellous industrial and social development of Occidental civilisation. He returned to his home land more impressed than ever with its needs of the elements which had made those nations so powerful and prosperous. Had he possessed this knowledge at the beginning of his public career, how much more valuable would have been the services to the country of this commanding personality, and how much greater the credit he deserves for having served it so well in ignorance of the great world beyond the confines of the Middle Kingdom.

The diary gives us new light upon his relations and personal intercourse with Their Majesties and especially with the Empress Dowager, Tze Hsi, that notable woman, who for half a century was the ruling spirit of the Chinese Government. At four different times in his career he was stripped of his "yellow jacket" and all his honours, and disgraced in the eyes of his countrymen by that irascible woman, yet he remained loyal to the Throne, assured that she knew the value of his services and would again bestow upon him honour and high duty. He records: "Whenever there is trouble, I am always the physician in attendance, but, instead of collecting a fee, I am usually subject to a fine for my trouble and skill."

On several occasions, when the fate of the nation
was in peril, although under the shadow of her dis-
pleasure, he did not hesitate to seek an audience
with the Empress Dowager. When the war party
had gained the ascendancy and hostilities were about
to be declared against Japan, he remonstrated so
strongly with her against the step that "Her Majesty
flew into the worst rage in late times," and sent him
away stripped of his insignia of honour. Again when
the Boxer outbreak was preparing, although he was
in retirement and without office, knowing that she
was falling under the influence of that movement,
he records, "I am leaving for Peking to-night, determined to see Tze Hsi herself, and present the situation to her in the plainest manner." A lengthy interview occurred, but it ended with the Empress
Dowager "alive with wrath and angry words" and
the Viceroy sent from the palace, never again to
appear in her presence. She was evidently committed
to the Boxer movement and he was powerless to
avert the calamity that was impending.

Notwithstanding the diary reveals the Empress
Dowager as an arrogant, cruel, and headstrong
woman, and the Emperor as a weakling, through all
vicissitudes the Viceroy remained faithful to the
Manchu Dynasty. When following the upheaval
and the siege of the legations the suggestion was
made in diplomatic circles and the press that the
reigning family be deposed and a new emperor placed
on the throne, he denounced it as so much idle talk,

and recorded in his diary, as he made known to the diplomatic corps, that there was no Chinese family sufficiently respected to rule the country in peace and order.

The last service he rendered his country was the crowning act of his long career. After the Empress Dowager and the Court had fled from the capital, as the allied armies occupied Peking and rescued the legations and foreign refugees, the nations which had been so grossly outraged instructed their diplomatic representatives to seek the punishment of the guilty officials and exact full indemnity for the losses sustained. Notwithstanding Li Hung Chang had been driven from her presence with angry words and banished to a distant province at Canton, from her hiding-place in the mountains she summoned him to Peking to meet the angry and determined diplomats, and save the throne from extinction and the empire from dismemberment.

Although the disease which brought him to the grave was rapidly undermining his strength, he made the long journey back to the capital. On his way, at Tientsin, he makes this entry in his diary: "I fear the task before me is too great for my strength of body, though I would do one thing more before I call the earthly battle over. I would have the foreigners believe in us once more, and not deprive China of her national life." His labours were successful, thanks in large measure to the high consideration shown him by the foreign negotiators. It is gratifying to Americans to know that in his diary he gives our Government great credit for aiding him to save his country from dismemberment and from conditions too burdensome to endure.

Within a few weeks after he signed the Protocol which gave his country peace, he ended his earthly life in the seventy-ninth year of his age. It was a fitting end to the stormy career of the greatest of Oriental statesmen, and one of the most distinguished of the public men of the world.

JOHN W. FOSTER.

May, 1913.

MEMOIRS OF
LI HUNG CHANG

CHAPTER I

HIS AMBITIONS IN LITERATURE

"SOME day I hope to be the Chang-yuan [the poet-laureate] of China."

These significant words, of such interest to the student of the life of Li Hung Chang, were written by him as early as 1846, while the industrious and brilliant young man was preparing for those higher examinations which he was to take a year later, when he would go up for the highest literary water-mark of his country —the Metropolitan or Third Degree of the Han-lin.

That honour he gained fully, and since he ranked among the three most successful in a total of four thousand, it may be assumed that, notwithstanding Western views of Chinese educational methods, he might rightly claim a place among the highly educated and gifted young men of his country and generation.

That his aspirations were lofty his own words tell, and that his industry and ability were in a very large degree of a kind making the attainment of his ambitions, in whatever channel they might tend, possible, no one who has followed his career of notable achievement and high recognition will gainsay.

Li's memoirs, the words he wrote from time to time, often carelessly, often with apparent haste, and again with a style and diction indicating diligent and laborious thought, all point to one supreme fact: that from the beginning of his school-days almost to the day of his death he cherished, above all others, the profession of literature, and that it was his hope to be known in the future story of his country as a poet, essayist, and historian.

"Some day I hope to be the poet-laureate of China," he wrote in 1846. "I am a newspaper man myself," he said to a New York reporter exactly fifty years later.

"*January*, 1846. — This day I completed the last of my examinations, and I know I have won the Ready-for-Office degree! I know, too, that I passed high, for I wrote and wrote with great ease; and the classics I can repeat word for word.

"I believe if the great Emperor Chow — oh! how great he was in learning and in the arts! — would submit me to an examination, I would please him by my answers. Yes, and some arts that have grown and flourished since his time, in which I would surprise him! He taught that all the six arts were necessary for a man's life and happiness, but he did not speak much of the classics, for the very good reason that the classics were not as important as now.

"The good King of Learning made music the first. I am deficient in that, for in these days it is not gentlemen who play in the streets nor sing at fairs. Archery I know little of, but it would come to me with slight practice, for in our family 2800 years ago, or 2900, — I shall figure this out, — a great ancestor, now among the chieftains of the Celestial Kingdom, was famous for his archery. He made the first bows in all Asia, drew them from the hearts of unknown trees, kept them for long weeks immersed in the brine of young sows, and turned them out the strongest and with the greatest accuracy of spring in all the world. I could practise archery now and become expert, but I do not want to become a soldier, and there is no hunting by which a young man could live in these days.

"The same in horsemanship. The horses are not used much. I mean there is only a horse to a league these days, and I do not expect to go north or west to ride camels. Besides, riding camels is not horsemanship.

"But in the other arts of Chow I know I would please him, just as I have pleased [here the young graduate gives a list of more than two hundred and seventy names] . . . with the progress I have made. In the memorising of the classics, in handwriting — my characters are clean and artistic, the most so in the college the doctors say — in mathematics, even into remote algebra, in astronomy, and in social and religious rites I am elated and confident. Astronomy

I shall study more and more; it, and pure literature, for who can be a great poet unless he understand the movements in the heavens, and know the planets and their orbits by name and rote?

"It is not given to any man to indite great classics merely because he is a graduate of the Third College [LL.D.], but if he have the education, and behind the education the love, and behind the love the desire and purpose, he can do work that will make his name live gloriously among his countrymen.

"I have all these now. I am between twenty-four and twenty-five years of age. My father is between forty-one and forty-two. That is a difference of seventeen. In such a length of time, if I do not suffer accident through the night, or am not set upon by ruffians in this brawly neighbourhood, and if the governor or viceroy give me a place under him, I shall do much to advance myself in my own esteem and in the esteem of others. People would laugh at me, perhaps, the students would stone me, and the professors and friends, especially [another long list of names] . . . might not think it possible, but some day I hope to be the Chang-yuan of China."

"*January* 27, 1846. — To-day I finished reading for the ninth time the fine lesser classics, 'Lieh Nu Chuen' [The Record of Cultured Women]. My list of books is not large, but I am making good use of those I have. Each time I peruse one thoroughly I make a note within it, with the time of beginning and the time of ending set down.

"This is one of the classics no part of which I have yet attempted to memorise; but there are many beautiful passages, and the record tells of such lovely and heroic women that it is most interesting. The story of Wha-Mou-Loh is most fascinating, and already I have begun some stanzas to her memory."

"*January* 28. — My people are bringing the matter of my marriage too earnestly before me. This is true more particularly of my uncle, quite more so than my father, for they are together in arranging a matrimonial alliance for me with a Sweet Blossom of Hoh-fei. The young woman is exceedingly virtuous, so far as I have been able to learn, and my mother vouches for her good in all things. And in her personal appearance there is everything to entice a young man who might have any desires for matrimony in his head. But an ancient saying is, 'Take a blossom early and some of the fruit of your life-tree is gone,' and it has impressed me greatly with its truth.

"It is not that I do not want this sweet maiden of respectable family. Her family is equal to ours in wealth and standing, but I am, as yet, not in a position to justify the beginning of a family — regardless of what my uncle may say, or of my prospective patrimony.

"I do not know, of course; but I am of the belief that my life will be a long one, and that sufficient opportunity will be given me to raise up fruit that will honour my memory. It is holy and right that one should beget many sons to love his memory and make great his grave, and on no account will I oppose the law and the religion.

" . . . My good chum, Ah Fing, called, and we had a long and serious conversation. He tells me that his most severe parent desires that he take as wife the child-daughter of the law-aunt at Po — that he has never seen her, does not wish to, and will soon start for the south.

"Ah Fing is a good young man, and full of industry and straight habits. He, too, believes he will follow the calling of literature, and he brought several long scrolls of romances which he has written since our days together when both were studying for the chu-jen [promoted scholar] degree. I could not hurt him so much as to tell him that while his romances seemed most interesting his language was too plain, and like the speech of the street people. I did, though, criticise his manuscript, for he writes a tsao tsz style [a sort of abbreviated character writing], and even that is homely and without grace. He was slightly put out, I fancy, when I exhibited to him some of my compositions in the best hing-shu, with elaborate ornament work and dainty colours in the high and left corners.

"It has always been my idea that carelessness

in any branch of art or work or even thought is bad. Perhaps it is egotistical for me to write in my own book this way about myself; but many, yes, thousands of men before me, have thus kept records of their lives, and have not hesitated to express their thoughts; and it is good to write down what one thinks. But Ah Fing's careless ways, together with the fact that he has no ink in his stomach [i.e., no literary ability], make it appear to me that he will make but a precarious living with his pen. I did not tell him so; for so many unkind things have been said to me, and they have cut so deeply, that it is not my purpose to make light of the attempts of others, nor to discourage them in their honest ambitions.

"But I hope that I shall never grow so careless as poor brother Ah Fing. Ah! if I had failed to pass the chu-jen, as he did — he even failed thrice in the Budding Genius examinations — I would have hidden my body in the hills or let it float in the river!"

"*March* 19. — There is bounding happiness in my inmost heart to-day, for I have been given a regular place in the office of the chi-fu [head] of the prefecture, and I know that my start on the right way to political progress has been made!

"My noble and severe parent also rejoices, and my mild mother is happy beyond compare. I do not know how my uncle feels, or whether he has yet

learned the glad tidings; but he will soon know, for
my father has gone in his chair to tell him, and to
invite him to a feast we will enjoy to-morrow.

"Perhaps I shall marry now. The Sweet Blossom
wants me, according to what she has told the go-
between, and also what her mother has said to
mine."

"*Late. Between the days.* — It has been impossible
for me to close an eye and keep it closed, so good
do my spirits feel over the fortunate tidings. Even
my uncle, in his home on the Hong road, heard the
news before my father had arrived, and had started
for our house with two fat geese and a fish. They
missed each other on the way, for father went on the
highroad by the fruit wall, while uncle took the
main Hong road direct to the yamen of the fu in
order to thank the latter and leave a present.

"Uncle is claiming that my good fortune is largely
due to him, owing to his intimate acquaintance with
the fu. He, himself, was a collector of liken for a
number of years.

"Of course I did not dispute my uncle, but
thanked him generously and upon my knees. Yet
every one roundabout knew that four days ago the
hein-kwan [district magistrate], the honourable
Pi-wang, sent for me, and spake the most encour-
aging words I have heard for many moons: —

"'Do you remember, Li, when you stole my
goslings from the Splendid Water Lake?'

"I told him that I remembered it well, though the wrong happened many years ago.

"'Do you remember the time you cast the cobble and nearly killed the little daughter of Wee, the one daughter he would not have die for anything?'

"I told him my memory was very good yet very sorrowful upon that affair. And I explained, as I had done before, that I was fighting with the Hop-e boy, and had no intention of hurting the little girl.

"'Well, Li,' continued the district magistrate, 'it was my opinion in those days that you would some day come to a ling-chi death [of a thousand slashes], and my heart was made glad when I saw you wince under the blows you received in punishment for those offences, and your father was in like manner pleased, for he avowed he had been unable to do much with you at his yamen.

"'But of late years your conduct, so far as we are aware, has been exemplary, and in your studies you have outstripped them all. Now, then, recite for me sixty and six paragraphs, commencing at the last, of the 'Spring and Autumn Annuals.'"

"How pleased I was that he had selected the great work which I could write off from beginning to end with a stick in the red sand. I recited off for him the sixty and six, and was still going on when he raised his hand and stopped me. Then it was that he told me he had wanted for some time to give me a place in the hein-kwan office, but he knew it was my father's desire that I start with the fu.

"Then, after I had thanked him with all my heart, both because he had forgiven my early wrongs — though stone-casting was not so to my discredit — and had interceded for me with the chi-fu, I came away, my soul magnified to the heavens. I knew the hien to be a most upright and open-hearted man, who very often spoke the truth, and I did not doubt at all but that the chi-fu would send for me with very little delay.

"And there has been great rejoicing at our house since I returned home, — so much so in my own case that I have been unable to sleep, and I am afraid my face looks like that of a man given to drugs. But all will be well after to-morrow, for I shall feast well and read some of my poetry to the assembled guests. I sent word to Ah Fing to come, but my mother has often scolded him when he has visited here, and he may not think he is welcome unless he brings a parcel of rice, which is impossible with the poor fellow; for at his home they believe themselves fortunate if they have meat twice during the winter, and maize-meal and vegetables the rest of the time."

Whether the youthful enthusiast and office-holder ever wrote an account of that feast is not known, but among the six hundred or more manuscripts of his which were and are at present in the possession of a grand-nephew at Nanking, and which were courteously submitted for the purposes of these translations, is a lengthy poem descriptive of such

an affair as he here tells us was about to occur.
Indeed the subject-matter and treatment are such
that there can be little if any doubt but that the
poem relates to the very occasion in question.

The poem *in toto* is rather too lengthy for reproduc-
tion here, and particularly as the latter portions of it
are so involved in thought relating to the realms and
times of the most ancient of the Chinese writers that
its rendition in literal English is very difficult. A
number of the stanzas, however, commencing with
the fifth, are here reproduced.

AN EARLY REWARD OF GENIUS

AND THE JOYOUS FEAST SENT BY THE GOOD GENII TO
THE YOUTH OF GREAT EXPECTATIONS

No questionings do mock my mind,
　That the good genii of the sky
Will favour those who hold quite true
　To all the rightful things.

These words I say because in recent day
　Sweet tidings, like water of the stream,
Have flowed into my heart to stay
　And make a lake of gladness there.

I sought the honours of the school and literati,
　I worked at morn, and midday too,
I strove when other students shirked,
　Or wasted time at games.

My heart did burst with learning's longing,
　Nothing else could give me joy.
I memorised and worked the harder
　To realise my fond desire.

The clouds in glory sent their rains
    To water seeds of thought in me:
The birds sang ever sweet refrains,
    Inspiring me to con sweet words.

Soon I became a Budding Genius,
    And then another rank I took,
And then the highest flight I gained:
    Thus I reached my heart's desire.

But when the hien-kwan of the district
    Sent for me to seek his yamen,
I hastened with my fears excited —
    How happily was I mistaken! .

O, what blessed words he uttered! —
    He who once had caused me pain —
Of how the whole hien rejoiced,
    And that an office now was mine.

Then came a time of song and feasting —
    Happy feasting in my home,
With father proud, and friends about me,
    Eating, drinking — rice and tea.

Glad and merry mandarins feasting!
    Joy within my heart was swelling,
For the honour that they showed me,
    For my parent's pride in me!

Then follow those parts already referred to, so
abstract and involved in thought and diction that
the translators were unable readily to render them
into English; and which appeared as a successful
attempt on the part of the enthusiastic young writer
to go beyond his depth.

CHAPTER II

IF all the writings of Li Hung Chang were to be fully translated, and the parts relating to the various subjects upon which, during a period of over half a century, he continued to express his views, were so segregated that his written comments might follow each other in regular and chronological order, it is to be doubted if a more entertaining subject than that of Christianity could be selected.

As stated in the Preface of this volume, it has been thought desirable to make, under various headings, such selections from the great mass of material received from the hands of the translators as would be in consonance with the chapter or part title, thus affording the reader a more concrete and at the same time comprehensive view of the subject treated by the author. Some of the great topics are, however, treated at such length in many entries of his diary, or in other papers wholly detached from any relationship with it, that the matter would fill a published volume. For instance, his writings concerning the Empress Dowager and the Court are estimated by competent authorities to be the equivalent of half a million English words. On the ever recurring subject of foreigners, missionaries, and Christianity, — he regards all foreigners as Christians, if not all Christians as foreigners, — the Viceroy seemed never to tire of writing, and it is likely that two volumes at least of a size similar to this could be filled with the transcriptions of such manuscripts.

The following selections, therefore, may be viewed as but a very small proportion of the large number of entries in his memoirs; yet they have been chosen with such discretion as to justify the belief that within the necessarily confined limits they indicate Li's feelings toward "foreigners and their religion" — feelings which were constantly shifting and changing — during a period of over fifty years.

The first mention of Christianity in his writings is found to have been made while he was looking for his doctorate of letters at the Imperial Han-lin College, Peking, in 1849: —

"I think it would be a noble and glorious career, and highly pleasing to the sacred gods and to my ancestors, if in all my books and papers I were to tell the people the truth about the sacred gods and false genii of the foreign devils. I could easily obtain the information which would show up these impostors to the whole people, at least to the base and ignorant coolies of the south, who, I hear, are listening to the sacrilegious utterances of the black-robed individuals.

"These foreign devils come to the country for no good to it. They preach and talk in loud voices, and hold up their hands, and pretend that they

come for the people's benefit; but I hear that each
and every one of them is a paid agent of some foreign power, and is here only to spy upon the Government.

"I hear that in the Far West for many years,
altogether by far too many, there have been numbers of these black-robes teaching their nefarious
doctrines, and uttering defiance to the Jade Emperor
and all the gods. These black-robes are of one sect
of the foreign devils, and I hear there are many sects,
all hating each other and all preaching for the same
god whom they call the Tien-fu [Heavenly Father].
If they have such a father he cannot be proud of his
sons, for they are unlearned men and barbarians.

"It is a part of their teaching that the Tien-fu let
his son come on earth and die for wicked people.
Such teaching! If they would say that he came and
died for the good people it would sound sensible,
even if the rest of their doctrines are too absurd for
a man with brains to give a serious thought to. If the
gods are good and want men to be good will they
allow members of their families to be killed like
criminals for the sake of criminals? It has been long
intimated that most of these foreign devils are
crazy, and I am beginning to believe it. But it is
strange that they should be able to draw any of our
people away from the old religion and old philosophy.
I cannot understand how it is, but I am sure this
crazy fad will die out."

Again, in 1849, he wrote: "Dr. Quong tells me that he has heard several of these foreign devils preach their insane doctrine in Honan. These were of that sect that hails from the country of the French, and are called the Tien-chu kiao [Roman Catholics]. These persistent demons have been over a century in the country, and they even grow queues, not only to fool the people but to try to fool the gods! They want to make believe they are Chinese, yet at the same time they would make fun of the religion of the people.

"These fanatics have some very queer ideas of their own. They say that more greatly to honour their god they abstain from having wives, not even one wife; and yet they urge the people to marry young, and to let all their children, girls as well, grow up. What kind of teaching is this? These fellows will die, and leave no one to mourn for them nor attend their graves. But I am wondering if none of this sect marry where their new preachers will come from. Perhaps they expect their fool converts to select preachers from their number that will not marry. And maybe they are right and will thus succeed, for when people are so twisted in their heads as to believe what these black-robes say, they may be ready to do as they do.

"Dr. Quong has once before written the Censors to memorialise the Throne for the extinction of the black-robes in the West, but the Chief Censor wrote in return that the Throne would not dignify the foreign sect by taking notice of it. Besides, it has been learned that the land of the French is a very strong kingdom far to the other end of Asia, and that these black-robes are all officers of the Government. Still, it is reported that they live off the people, and yet do not have yamens or fine houses. And their temples are great buildings, square and ill-looking, but well built."

The author does not appear to have written much concerning the Christians during the next few years, but his vigour and apparent hatred, as shown by a lengthy entry in his diary, made in 1854, rather make up for the seeming delinquency. He is again in central China, holding office; and the Taiping rebels, calling themselves Christians, — without at all knowing the meaning of the term nor practising in even the remotest degree its teachings, — are marching through the central coast provinces with fire and sword.

"Why do not all our people rise together and drive these enemies from the country? I did not think the ideas of the cursed foreigners would ever take hold of a large number, but it appears that in the south there are thousands and thousands of mongrels who are willing to follow the smell of this Hung Siu-tsuen dog, who has imbibed the bold doctrines of the other nations. Not only are they devastating the whole country, but they are forcing their beliefs upon the people everywhere. And, if reports are true, thousands more of the fanatics are preparing to come from Canton and the regions to the north.

"I have learned from good reports that in Nanking the Long-Haired Rebels have cut the heads off of many hundreds, and the ears of ten thousand who did not join at once in their vile beliefs. And this is the manner of acting of the members of the Association for the Worship of God (Shangti hwui), who are presuming to call this country the Kingdom of Heaven (Tien Kwoh).

"I do not think the authorities are half severe enough with these fanatics, and it is very wrong to take any of them into the Imperialistic forces when they surrender and declare repentance. They do not repent, the hounds! They are rats of disease caught from the leprous missionaries of Canton, and they would run into all the holes of the centre and north and spread their vile malady. The lingering death should be applied to all those who have countenanced this foreign doctrine, or in any way aided the marauders, though they may not have marched with them. If my own arms were not so lame during this season from rheumatism and other ailments of the blood, which I hope will soon pass, nothing could please me better than to take a place as executioner of the vermin. As it is, I am doing my share; for to help collect moneys for the support of our patriotic soldiers is in itself a great task, especially as the fertile fields have been so largely destroyed by these marauders."

About this time Li wrote: —

It is truly the greatest sacred duty
Of all patriotic sons of the Middle Kingdom,
And all who bow to the mighty Throne, —
The glorious seat of ten thousand years, —
To strike to the black heart
The Long-Haired bandits;
And to let out their vitals upon the earth,
That the swine of our gutters
And the fowls of the barnyards
And the mongrel curs of the alleys
May lick up their blood and gnaw their bones.

These fierce Long-Hairs are wild in their heads.
They have crazy notions of Heaven.
They have a new god
And his Elder Brother
Whom they follow to deeds of darkness.
They have forsaken all our sacred gods,
And spat upon the images,
And upon the graves of our ancestors.
They are dogs of low order,
Devils of blackest darkness,
Lepers of the foulest ills,
Serpents with marks of the pox,
Fowl that limp with gangrene!
They are not men at all in human shape,
Nor in their minds — for such are gone;
Nor in their new speech,
For they ape the tones of the foreign masters
And talk loud, like barking dogs at night.

Let them be given no quarter!
It is a great work and blessing
To pluck out their lying tongues,
To burn deep the sockets of their eyes,
To rip open their vile bellies,
To rub salt into many cuts,

To trim close their ears,
To draw forth the nails,

.   .   .   .

To bury deep whilst yet alive,
To use the pole upon their skulls.
Oh! all patriotic sons of the Middle Kingdom,
Drive these rank fiends
Into the salty sea,
Or make their rotting bones
Manure the land!

In 1865, two years after the capture of Nanking and the complete collapse of the Taiping Rebellion, Li Hung Chang at Suchau (Soochow) writes as follows:—

"It is always well for a man to give continued and serious consideration to a question before arriving at a final decision, and I find this particularly true with relation to the underlying character of the Taiping Rebellion. During the most of those long and bitter years I was wholly of the opinion that the foreigners along the coast, especially at Shanghai, Hong-Kong, and Canton, were in a very large measure responsible for the outbreak of the Long-Haired Rebels, but I am now forced to the conclusion that my thoughts and opinions were very wrong.

"This I have learned in a number of ways, mostly since the fall of Nanking. Yet I remember that upon at least one occasion General Gordon, who was my lieutenant-commander of the 'Ever Victorious Army,' tried to explain to me the doctrines of the Christian Church; but I would not listen in patience, so much had I learned to hate the name. Gordon at that time would have me believe that none of the Christian nations were in sympathy with the Long-Hairs; and he offered as partial proof of the truthfulness of his words the fact that his own nation, which he said was the leading Christian country of the world, was at that very time lending all due aid to China for the suppression of the rebellion.

"I remember Gordon's words very well, as they were translated by ——, for Gordon himself could not speak fully in our language. But it so happened that this was about the time that General Ching accused Gordon, to me, of being in communication with the Wangs of the Taipings, and for a greater or shorter period I did not know whether to believe him or not. Because of this feeling of mine — which I afterwards learned was entirely wrong, and a very great injustice to the fine loyalty of General Gordon — I all the more doubted the sincerity of his words, and believed it was simply a case of one Christian endeavouring to be of some assistance to another.

"But since I have been Governor, and since peace has given time for many things which for a number of years I could not enjoy, I have taken opportunity to inquire diligently into the training and so-called inspiration of Hung Siu-tsuen, with the result that I have ascertained that the leader of the Taipings was as far from being a Christian as I from a Tartar, and that neither he nor his followers had any conception of how the Western Church members live in peace or fight in war. I have even seen the

brother of the foreign devil missionary, who gave
Siu-tsuen his first lessons, and he has told me that
his reverend brother gave no encouragement to
Siu-tsuen or any of his followers to make a study of
the Christian books.

"Yet, it was the loud words of these Long-Hairs
that gave us the strongest impression, and that at
the same time brought them hundreds of thousands
of followers in the four provinces. In all their
marches, pillages, and battles they called upon the
name of the foreign devils' god to give them victory
and to send them many new recruits. And they had
such great success in the early years, and so many
hundreds of thousands believed in the divine appointment of the leader, that I myself began to believe
that they were real Christians as they claimed, and
that their so-called Heavenly Father and his Elder
Brother [God and Jesus Christ] were giving them aid
and encouragement. It was difficult for me to believe
that our own gods and good genii had forsaken the
religion of the Middle Kingdom, and departed from
their guardianship of the Throne; but with the
continued success of the rebels I began myself to
lose some little part of my former faith, and even
to question whether our illustrious ancestors were
still in love with the people who worshipped them.
Thus it was that from day to day, especially in those
terrible years when the Long-Hairs were sweeping
all before them and assembling armies that were
larger by far than any of those which the Imperial

Government might master, I hated the foreign religion more violently than all other scourges in the world; and I prayed and hoped that not alone would the Taipings be destroyed, but that earthquakes, eruptions of mountains, and terrible fevers would make the Christian nations without a man, a woman, or a child.

"But I have learned many things by studying this matter. First of all I have come to the conclusion that it is not best for a man to pronounce hurried judgments upon matters to which he has not given diligent and continuing examination. It is well for a man to forget many things, and when he seeks a clear and unbiassed opinion upon some certain matter, to begin to look at it as if he knew nothing at all before. Then when facts and theories are presented to his mind — it is better to have facts, for theories change with the sun and the moon — he may stand them up like culprits before a magistrate, pick out the good and the substantial, and decapitate the remaining ones.

"Since my present office began I have had more intercourse with foreigners than in all my life before, and I cannot assert truthfully that they have played greater tricks on me than my own countrymen; but this may be more because of their pride than their honesty, for, as I understand it, the citizens of most of these European nations take a pretended delight in evincing a superiority over the Asiatics, and are therefore opposed to doing many things when they

are away from their home lands which they would
not hesitate at all to do in the places of their birth.

"In this I do not see any true moral philosophy,
but rather a weakness in their attempt to impress
grandly what they believe to be weaker nations.
I am told that great numbers of the foreigners along
our coasts, especially in Shanghai, Hong-Kong, and
Macao, left their homes because they owed large
sums of money, and either could not pay or did not
care to. Yet these same foreigners, when they are
residents of Asian ports, will be angry with their
coolies and servants if they are not on hand promptly
to receive wages due them. I cannot believe they
are very angry; at least if they are it is entirely senseless, for, if the man who has performed the labour
is in no hurry for his pay, does it cost the foreigner
anything to hold it a day or two for him? If held two
months or two years, is not the interest all the greater?

"The British officials from Shanghai have impressed me most favourably since I have held high
office, and I have often wished that I might be able
to speak their language. Some of them converse
very well in Mandarin, and one or two of the secretaries write it very well; but these latter are those
who have been many years along the coast.

"All these tell me that the Christian people in
foreign lands were rejoiced that the Taipings failed
in their rebellion, but I have had translations made
from some of the articles in the English press, and it
would seem as if the editors were themselves going

to die because of the treatment accorded some of the Long-Hairs. And I find that in nearly all foreign quarters I am severely blamed for what happened to the Wangs at Suchau, and am called a 'Yellow Barbarian'! I will no longer attempt to answer these outside attacks: all I will say is that I did not give an order for the execution of the Wangs, but had I done so I would not have regretted it very sorely, for their going gave the greatest pleasure to the Emperor and the Empress Dowager, and the country was well served. If General Gordon, during any of his visits to the Taiping leaders, made certain promises to them, he was exceeding any authority ever given him."

Receiving in June, 1870, word from Peking that he should prepare to go north as Commander of the Forces and Viceroy of Chihli Province, Li wrote: —

"I am not too highly pleased with this new appointment, for I am quite at home and satisfied where I am; but in the Province of Chihli there are just now the worst elements in the empire so far as the treatment of foreigners is concerned, and I am happy to know that the Throne believes my hand strong enough to cope with these ruffians.

"It cannot be said, even by my worst foes, that I have been a bosom friend to the foreigner, either the man that comes to force his trade upon us, or the fellow who would cram his religion down our throats. Of course it is offensive to our educated people to know that these churchmen are sent from all parts of the world to explain to us the nicest way to live and the happiest way to die, but the entering wedge was inserted many years ago, and it is now too late to cry out against what we once permitted. We opened our gates and the goats came in, and now the goatherds insist that the pasture wherein their hungry flocks have so long grazed shall not be taken from them.

"Yet, in spite of all our 'dislikes, if we truly have the best interests of China at heart, we will no longer oppose the coming of the foreigner, whether he be trader, missionary, or tourist; for he is bound to come anyway, even if he must ride behind a bayonet, or sit upon the big gun of a warship. And it is just as well, much better in fact, that all our people come to a realisation of this.

"Just now, in the Province of Chihli, there is a great agitation among certain classes against the French priests and nuns; and, in fact, against every agent of a foreign institution. But Their Majesties desire an end put to all such things, and I feel highly complimented to think that I am regarded as the proper person to put Their Majesties' desires into effect. I shall spare none of these ruffians and hard-heads when I am at my post; and if the foreign element in the population, whether priests or harlots, missionaries or opium fiends, does not get protection it will be because the sword and the bamboo are worn to soft places.

"When last I saw Tseng-kofan we spent several hours in full discussion of this great problem — a problem which, unless settled in the right way, will be as a dagger ever likely at a moment's notice to be thrust into the body of the nation. Tseng-kofan, like myself, has changed his views exceedingly in the past five or six years, and is no longer a hater of the Christians. He told me that it was his intention some of these days to memorialise the Throne to issue an edict of complete toleration for all foreigners of whatever profession or occupation, and I told him that I would gladly join in such a memorial if he would so desire."

"*June* 13. — Though my action may not be fully understood I am writing an article upon the rights of foreigners to reside in China and prosecute their own affairs without insult or hindrance. I hope to have it ready to present to General Tseng-kofan, who is soon to have an audience with Her Majesty, the illustrious old Buddha, when he may have opportunity to leave it with her for her private counsel. If the Court will give sanction I will have many thousand coipes printed at my own expense, and circulated in every province. I think there is scarcely anything I could do at the present time that would result in greater good to both foreigners and Chinese."

In an entry made some weeks later, Li mentions

that his memorial on behalf of foreigners was not completed, "because I hope soon to speak directly with Her Majesty, when I shall seek permission to write my views upon this all important matter."

"*Viceroy's Yamen, Tientsin, June 23.* — The hell leaders of this city, following out their own cursed notions, have again brought China into disrepute with the whole world, and humiliated the Throne; but these ignorant fiends who incite or take part in outrages must not think that they will escape the penalty, for I shall see to it that every miscreant who had aught to do with the massacre of two nights ago will get his just dues."

"*June 24.* — The acting French Consul called upon me early to-day presenting a note from the French Minister at Peking, asking what steps I was taking to apprehend and punish the participants in the outrages upon the Consul, the Catholic priests, nuns, and converts.

"This is the way the foreign official acts in China! An English trader's shop window is no more than broken by some rowdies than the Consul or the Minister is at the yamen demanding to know what we are going to do about it. A French dandy gets into a street brawl with a band of ignorant coolies, and before the officials have even heard that such an affair took place the Consul or Minister is shaking his fist at the Viceroy. A fat, red-faced German, half

full of stout beer and smelling of cheese, falls into a
gutter and breaks one of his legs. Passers-by try to
help him to his feet, and he thinks they are going to
rob him. He pulls a revolver and shoots a native,
and then friends of the latter throw stones and cut
the fat German's red face. Immediately his Consul
or his Minister is knocking loudly at the door of the
yamen and demanding 'satisfaction' for the 'insult
offered the German flag'!

"Thus it is in China. If that same Englishman or
Frenchman or German had the same sort of trouble
in his own country he would be well satisfied if
a policeman and a Justice of the Peace took any
notice of his case; but in China he expects and
demands that the whole machinery of his Government be invoked to bring the 'Yellow Barbarian' to
terms!

"Of course I do not mean to bring up these cases
in comparison with the present vile outrage; but it
is an injury to my pride to think that the French
Minister and the French Consul should demand to
know what I am 'going' to do when any one of
any intelligence in Tientsin and Peking, themselves
included, knows how sternly I view all infractions of
the law, and in particular outrages against foreigners.

"I said to the French official: 'You will please
pardon me, Mr. Consul, but if you will inquire at
the prison you will find what I have already *done* in
the matter. And if you will inquire of almost any
coolie in the city you will be told that more than

three thousand soldiers are scouring the whole of
the province and every corner and hole of Tientsin
to bring suspected ones before the authorities.'

"The Consul in one way was greatly pleased with
my answer, although I only imparted information
such as was already in his possession; but he desired
to impress me with the importance of his position as
representative of the great French nation, forgetting
that I myself am the virtual ruler of as many people
as there are in twenty cities like Paris, where Mr.
Consul would not be known upon the streets."

(No date.) — "Having fixed the time for the
execution of the ringleaders in the massacre I have
been requested by both the French and Russian
Ministers to postpone the decapitations. They are
desirous of being present to witness the show, or,
more truly, to see that the culprits really die after
their heads are chopped off.

"This is another disgusting trait of the foreigners,
and these messages of to-day have caused me much
annoyance. Perhaps they think that in all my words
and actions against such outrages I am only looking
for effect, whereas, if they would know the truth, I
am more anxious to see such vagabonds put out of
the way than are any of the foreign Government
representatives in Peking or Tientsin. It is not only
right on mere grounds of revenge or satisfaction for
the lives of the men, women, and children taken,
but it is necessary for the good of China that swift

and sure punishment be meted out to all offenders.
If my son or daughter were killed in Europe or
America I believe the authorities would see to it that
the murderer or murderers paid the penalty. And
it will be so here in Chihli so long as I am Viceroy.

"Of course most of our people think that a Chinese
young woman who would wish to go into a foreign
nation among strangers deserves to be killed by a
mob, or have some fatal accident befall her; but the
views of the English and Americans and other Christian nations are very different. While our people
think the putting out of the way of the nuns is a
benefit to the latter — for they have no husbands,
and by their looks do not eat much — as well as to
the world at large, in France, as the Consul says,
these women are looked upon as great and holy
saints in the next world. And, is n't this strange? —
they were nothing but plain, hard-working women,
looking after a lot of children (of whom it is a pity
they did not die in infancy), when the work of a crazy
band of fanatics makes holy saints and immortal
ancestors of them. Yet, for this great transformation,
as I understand the present temper of that nation,
the French are ready to send a fleet and an army to
kill as many thousand Chinese as get in their way.
And France is a Christian nation. I do not understand in full the application of the doctrines they
profess to believe, nor the principles they announce
themselves willing to uphold."

"*July* 21. — Again the date for the execution of the criminals connected with the massacre of the French consular officer and the Christians has been postponed, this time also upon request of the Russian Minister. Yet the Foreign Office is continually hearing that in Paris and St. Petersburg the Governments are impatient with the delay in bringing these outragers to punishment. What does all this mean? Are Russia and France looking for some excuse to make war upon China?

"It has been brought to my attention by one of the British consular officers of this city that it is very probable that France would declare war upon us if it were not for the fact that she is just now very much occupied with Germany. I do not know whether to believe this or not, but I understand that the same report has reached the Tsung Li Yamen at Peking from another source. If this is so it is very wrong on the part of the French, for the rioters would have paid the penalty of their crime days ago had it not been for the request of the French Minister. This appears strange, and not at all as it should be.

"The Minister has himself assured me that he is thoroughly satisfied with my attitude in the entire matter, but in the same breath he did complain unofficially of what he terms the 'apathy of the Imperial Government.' I explained to him that neither the Throne, the Court, nor the Government Departments at the capital had anything to do with the punishment of the outragers; that I had been given a wholly free hand in the entire matter, and that I would see that each guilty one was brought to book in the most certain and summary manner if I was not interfered with by the Legations. I asked the Minister himself to set a date for the executions, but he declined to do this."

"*July* 25. — Lying and contemptuous officials, I believe, are often at the bottom of these riots against foreigners. In the past I have been willing to believe the mandarins as a general thing exerted themselves vigorously to prevent anti-foreign outbreaks, but upon investigating this terrible massacre of a foreign official and so many church workers, and considering facts of some other recent outrages, I am convinced that shallow-minded and venial-hearted district and prefectural officers are largely to blame.

"I know that by so doing I will make hundreds and perhaps thousands of enemies throughout the country; but at my next audience with Her Majesty I am going to urge with all my strength, and as far as I dare proceed, that an edict be issued to the effect that fu and hein officials will be held personally responsible, in life and property, for the lives and property of Christians. If this is done there will be fewer attacks upon missions, and the missionaries will be allowed to pursue their vocations without hindrance."

"*July* 27. — General Tseng-kofan has issued a fine statement relieving the priests and nuns of any culpability in giving cause for the late massacre. He condemns the work of the mad rioters in the most scathing terms, and declares that the Throne is ever against such action on the part of its subjects, and is desirous of having the most condign punishment inflicted.

"I am happy that this action has been taken by Tseng-kofan, and it pleases me beyond measure to know that Their Majesties are willing to uphold me in the severe measures which I am taking to suppress anti-Christian lawlessness, and the still more drastic action I am ready to take if such appears necessary.

"It is my intention to end this rioting business in the Province of Chihli, if personally I must visit the magistrates and army officials at Peking, Paoting-fu, and Tientsin each week of my stay in office. The whole world will get the impression that our nation is indeed one of 'yellow barbarians' if these inexcusable and terrible affairs continue. I shall certainly memorialise the Throne for an edict, and at the same time I will make of my province a safe place in which foreign merchants and missionaries and their families may reside."

"*August* 23. — My heart is pierced with sorrow to-day to learn of the dastardly assassination of General Ma Yu-k'un, the great Viceroy of Nanking

— a man I was proud to call friend. It is too bad, altogether deplorable; and I pray the fiendish assassins will not only be made to pay for their deed by a lingering death, but that the spirits of the ancestors will rend their spirits into bits as small as flashes from diamonds.

"Perhaps some of my enemies will regard Viceroy Ma's taking-off as a lesson to me; for he was ever friendly toward the foreigners and their religion, and it was because of this feeling, no doubt, that he met death in the very height of his powers and use-fulness. Glorious man! — he paid with his life for the liberality of his mind and the openness of his heart. I wonder if the foreigners will really appreci-ate the sacrifice of this life in their behalf? Time will tell us.

"But if there are any who think that my own actions, much less my thoughts and feelings, will be influenced by the assassination of the Nanking Viceroy they are not acquainted with Li Hung Chang. On the contrary, the wild ruffians of Chihli will be dealt with more rigorously than ever. I will drive such fisticuffs and murderers out of my vice-royalty — if the Court does not interfere.

"Glorious Viceroy Ma Yu-k'un! He died for China, yet as a Chinese Martyr to the God of the Westerners!"

"*August* 25. — During the entire night I dreamed only of the dead Nanking Viceroy, and I saw his

cold body in the hands of the murderers. I do not
know when I have felt so ill as to-day. I shall deny
myself even to the agent of the Russian Minister,
who is to call."

"*September* 4. — The Grand Council has asked
me if the number of rioters awaiting execution for
the massacre cannot be reduced somewhat. This
interference is as bad or even worse than that exercised by the Legations. I have answered that I see
no way of exculpating any of the prisoners, but rather
that I am straining every effort to increase their
number. It would be well for the Grand Council
and the other high officials to be busying themselves
regarding the payment of the indemnity that is
demanded, and leave to me the details of dealing
with these hardened rascals."

"*September* 5. — I have pardoned one of the nine-
teen condemned to death. He is a low creature, and
would be happier and better in the ground than on
top of it. But I permitted him to tell his story again
this morning, having him brought into my presence
accompanied by one of the French priests, who,
luckily for himself, was at Tung-Chow at the time
of the Tientsin outbreak. The low creature explained
that he had been employed by the Sisters of Mercy
about the Orphanage, and that instead of being a
part of the original mob he himself was threatened
with death if he did not take a hand in the mad and
fiendish work.

"'Did you murder or burn?' I asked him.

"'No, Your Excellency, I did not; I made my escape as soon as I could, and then went to my home in the old city as quickly as possible.'

"'Are you a convert to Christianity?' I questioned.

"'Oh, no, Your Excellency, never, never!'

"When he made this answer the priest looked at the fellow reproachfully, and told him that he knew he was lying, and that instead of denying his faith he should be willing to die for it. Then the low creature, ashamed of himself, told me that he really was a convert.

"'Well, it is good for you that you have acknowledged it,' I told him, 'for I would not want to be accused of executing a Christian — even a worthless cur like yourself. I will, therefore, excuse you from decapitation; but you are sentenced to eternal banishment from this Middle Kingdom and its outer provinces. I hope you will seek a home in some Christian country, and that the Christians, as I doubt not they will, will find without delay a reason for killing you.'

"The low fellow then begged that the original sentence be carried out, and the priest said he did not much care. But I sent the liar and coward away, with an order that he be exiled from the whole coast. Such mendacious creatures as he would have a monster lie in his throat at the time of the falling of the sword, and the edge of the instrument would be dulled to a greater damage than his carcass would be worth."

On September 16 the Viceroy of Chihli wrote his last comment upon the massacre which for many months threatened to bring on a war between France and China, but regarding the satisfactory settlement of which the French Government made an announcement before the end of the year — a "Christmas present of peace," as the Republic's Minister expressed it.

Viceroy Li wrote: "Christian ministers, priests, and Sisters of Mercy preach peace and good will, and by their lives and works among the people indicate that they are honest in their intentions, and would show good example to their converts. But they have one great fault: it is unknown that they ever appeal directly to the local authorities when affairs do not go in a manner to please them. In the smaller villages they do not think of going to the head man of the place with their troubles, nor to the hein-kwan, nor the fu, nor the Governor, nor the Viceroy. But always they would air their griev- ances to the Consul, and the Consul to the Minister. This latter official — and I say it with all personal and official respect, for the Ministers are usually men of high standards — cables the trouble to his own Government oftentimes before bringing the mat- ter to the attention of ours. Thus it is that the journals in foreign parts publish the news of the

latest "Chinese outrage upon Christians," and the
people are ready to believe that our entire nation is
in arms against the foreigner. Two or three ruffians,
or half a hundred crazed fanatics who consider
themselves patriots — damn them! — give a bad
name to the whole empire, from the Throne to the
coolies.

"I am weary advising the missionaries as to the
best course to pursue in the event of trouble of whatever nature that concerns their lives and the prose-
cution of their labours; yet it is simply and solely
to make the acquaintance of the local officials, and to
have faith that the latter will accord full protection
against violence. If they have good reason to doubt
the sincerity or reliability of the local mandarins, or
the fu or hein magistrates, they should put themselves directly under the care of the Governor or
Viceroy. These latter may not love or admire the
missionary and his work to any greater extent than
does the fu or the hein, but they have more at stake
in the losing of their positions, and are generally
men of greater intelligence, broadmindedness, and
wealth.

"But to-day I personally witnessed the paying of
a debt in blood for the Orphanage massacre and the
killing of the French consular officer, and I am
pleased that this miserable chapter has been
brought to a close. The foreign Governments were
all represented at the scene, and I trust they are
satisfied. Sixteen heads were lopped off. The other

thirty-three culprits were started upon their journeys
into exile.

"I asked the French Minister if he was satisfied.

"'Yes, perfectly,' he answered. 'And how about
Your Excellency?'

"I told him that in a sense I was quite pleased,
but that there were still many 'rough necks' in the
province which needed a shaving by the 'heavy
razor.' I was thinking also of General Ma when I
spoke."

On February 17, 1886, this entry is found: —

"I am more and more convinced that the Christian
religion is not so much hated in itself, but that the
animosity which is found to a greater or lesser extent
throughout China against the 'foreign devils' is
because they are 'foreign.'

"During several years I have given quite careful
study and thought to the religion of the West, and
I cannot see that it is in conflict at all with our
own philosophy. On the contrary, the teachings of
Confucius and the doctrines of Jesus appear to be on
one exalted plane, conceived and promulgated for the
betterment of all mankind, 'heathen' and Christian.
I know this: that if my lot in life were cast in England, France, or America I should want to call myself a Christian, for that is the religion of those
countries; and a man who would order his life by its
tenets would keep out of trouble and be respected.
He would not think of Confucius, because he would
have no need for him or his teachings. And it is the

same way, reversed, in China: I have no need for Christ if I will but follow our own great sage and philosopher. But simply because I feel no personal call for the Christian religion I will not therefore oppose it, since I believe that there are thousands, perhaps millions, in China who would be somewhat benefited by a knowledge of Jesus, especially as they trouble themselves not at all to follow in the ways directed by Confucius.

"Therefore I would sum up the feelings of the more intelligent officials and literati to-day — for my own sentiments appear to be largely shared by this class in all the Eastern provinces from Canton to the Northern Capital — it is the foreigner who is disliked, not because of his religion, but because he is otherwise feared. He is feared not at all in this year because he may be the agent of Jesus Christ or a follower of that great man, but as a possible enemy to the political and industrial independence of the country.

"That this conclusion is correct I know from this one fact, regardless of any others: the Japanese are the most despised of all the foreigners, yet we Chinese know that they are not Christians, nor have they any of the good traits of the Christian nations, government, or people. Quite the contrary. The Japanese are very much like ourselves in matters of religion, philosophy, and ethics, yet we hate them and they despise us. Though they received all they have in arts, literature, and science from China, they pretend to be much better than we; and, instead of thanking China for all she has done for them, they would pluck her feathers from neck to tail, and, if opportunity offered, run off with the whole bird.

"Knowing these things and thinking of them as I do, and fully appreciating what the Christian nations did for us in a late emergency, I cannot say that I am not friendly to the people of the West, whether they come as merchants or missionaries, or do not come at all. And it is time that our people in the south and centre and north realise that all foreigners are not the same, and that some Christians are much to be preferred to some Taoists and followers of Buddha."

CHAPTER III

THROUGH attracting the attention of the famous scholar and soldier Tseng-kofan, at that time commander-in-chief of the regular and irregular forces employed against the Taipings in Central China, Li Hung Chang, then a comparatively obscure but brilliant civil officer of his native Province of Anhuei, was first engaged in the profession of arms; an occupation which was eventually to bring him into contact with General Charles Gordon and establish a relationship whose varying degrees of friendship and trust, at least on Li's side, are, during a number of years, told in notations of sufficient comprehensiveness to make a volume in themselves.

Quite with the enthusiasm of early youth, although he was thirty-five years of age, he writes of Viceroy Tseng-kofan in 1855: —

"It is the highest compliment of my life, and praise of my humble work in the different minor offices I have filled, to hear that the great Tseng-kofan has decided to give me a place under him in the extermination of the Chang-mao-tseh (Long-Haired Rebels). I am as yet uninformed as to the exact nature of my duties, but whatever they are I will do my best to fulfil them properly. Oh, I will fight — fight — fight, for I despise these rough

rebels who would go through the country like bands
of robbers. They would destroy the whole Government if they could, and would march to Peking and
level the Sacred Throne itself. But we must completely annihilate them, and drive them into the sea,
or feed their bodies to the swine upon the land.

"My father, who has been thrice to see Tseng-
kofan, says that but few men of China of late centuries have been greater scholars than the Viceroy.
What a reputation! Is it not wonderful to be learned
and profound in the classics, and at the same time
a wise administrator and soldier of great strategy.?
Yet such is Tseng-kofan — learned, wise, rigorous,
and brave! And such a man as this, whose deeds are
heralded and praised from the far south to the far
north, from Tibet to the eastern sea, desires me to
assist him in his great work.

"Tseng-kofan's family is like our own in many
ways, though it is necessary that I show a little
modesty, and do not draw the comparison too closely.
But his is one of the old Chinese families of Anhuei
and Kiangsu, for there are two great branches. It
was said by friends of mine that he came originally
of the Manchu blood, and that it was on this account
that he had been given high offices and vast prefer-
ments, but I have learned that this information is
wholly wrong, and that for eleven centuries the home
of the family has been in the provinces.

"1855. — Three of my old friends of student days
were with me to dine last night. They all came to

the office [Li refers very likely to the office wherein he was engaged as sub-treasurer of Hofei] during the day with the intention, as I soon saw, of chaffing me and disturbing my work. This was very wrong of them, for if they are not taken up with serious matters themselves, they should not make it a part of their business to interfere with the weighty affairs of others.

"P'ing remarked upon my good clothes and the heavy jade ring. I did not like what he said to the effect that my father must be more liberal these days than when I was studying for my degrees. I told P'ing I did not like his manner of speech, for it more than intimated that I was receiving no salary or, perhaps, that I was securing funds that did not rightly belong to me.

"It is true that both my father and my uncle are more liberal in their offers than they were six or eight years ago, and that I could obtain, if I needed, goodly sums from them. But it is not because they have changed in money matters; they know now that a borrowed sum could be quickly repaid with goodly interest, while before there would have been some uncertainty about it.

"I have not had as yet vast experiences in the world, but it is an established thought with me that if you are possessed of a definite amount of anything, people are willing to aid you to add to it, while if you are wholly without, it is a remarkable man who will offer you anything. It appears to be the same in

regard to all things connected with life. If a student
fails in the examinations none of the bachelors or
doctors will sit up nights with him in his recitations,
nor explain the difficult passages. But let him be
high in his student work, and come out at the head of
his lists in his examinations, and all the learned men
will offer their assistance to make him better. If a
man have no money at all, and is a ragged beggar
upon the highway, he is most likely to remain so,
for he has no friends, except mendicants like himself,
and they are of no use to him when he would buy a
bowl of soup on a cold night or a dish of locusts or
bees on a holiday. This rule extends even to the
affairs of the domestic realm, for if a man has gone
over a limit of years without a wife, all the women
of his district believe either that he cannot get one,
or that he would be unable to support one if he had
her. But when he is once married, and has assumed
a position of some standing in the community, there
are many women who think their daughters might
be valuable additions to his household."

"P'ing, San, and Klun are good friends of mine,
but I do not care to have them obtrude their noses
and tongues into my affairs when I am at the office.
The treasurer was not there when they called. Had
he been, he would have put a sudden stop to their
gibes, and ordered them to go about their own concerns. But, nevertheless, he heard of their visit, and
questioned me about it when he returned from the

office of the Chi-fu. He asked if I was making the yamen a place for reunions with my literati friends. Tsung is himself an ignorant man in all things literary, although he is a master of accounts and gives the collectors no rest. During the term of office few taxes have remained unpaid except in those districts which have been most greatly despoiled by the Taipings, and in such districts the Viceroy has always been considerate enough to allow of their being remitted."

"My friends, who have learned of the military appointment, never seem to tire with their jokes on my former ambition. Some of them who heard me say at one time that it was my hope to write a great classic, an epic that would perhaps give me high rank among the literary names of our history, have told of my aspirations all about; and even Tseng-kofan, in his talk with my father, asked by way of amusement if I would be a better officer with the dictionary or the sword. Of course, he was only uttering a playful jest, and my father knew it; for the Viceroy has told that his attention was first called to me by the statement made by the hein-kwan that I had stood so high in my literary work. Then when I wrote to him asking for an appointment, he complimented me highly upon the appearance of my manuscript — with which, in truth, I took extra pains. Later, when I saw him personally, he announced that all my record and accomplishments

were in my favour, and that he would appoint me to
a place near him; and that, if I deserved it, a promotion to a place of greater responsibility would
follow."

"Everybody knows that a 'soldier is despised,'
and that, according to the Old Rules, I am leaving
the greatest of the professions for the worst of occupations. At least, such would be the case if I were
going low in the ranks of a regiment or army that
fights alone for pay. It is not so in this case. I do
not like the occupation of arms, but I have my future
to think of, and the provinces need good men. I
have never left and will not leave the profession of
letters, but is this a time for writing poetry? Who
would read my stanzas and lines? Who cares for romances when fire and sword are in the district?
"It is wrong to say that I have forsaken the literati,
and that I have changed all my ambitions. Is not
Tseng-kofan the most learned scholar in all Central
China, and is he not Commander-in-Chief of all the
Forces?"

During the following years Li Hung Chang wrote
with even more care than was his practice, but of
matters relating largely to his own rise in the esti-
mation of the Viceroy, and consequent promotion
from one post to another. His diary and other
memoranda are filled with multitudinous detail, all
indicating that the "Ready-for-Office" graduate was

indeed "in office," and committed to a career of tireless political activity.

It appears that in the five years following the surrendering of his fiscal position, the young man had quite forgotten that "soldiers are despised," for a lengthy writing made in August contains the following: —

"To be selected as head of a great number of troops is indeed an honour not to be despised. It was my own banner [regiment] which first attracted the most favourable attention of the Commander-in-Chief, and has finally caused him to select me as head of the forces at Kiangsu. I did not expect the promotion, but it did not come as a great surprise, for my troops have been driving the Long-Haired Rebels (Chang-mao-tseh) before them, like chaff before the wind.

"In my earlier days I did not believe that I should enjoy engaging in battle or the sight of carnage; but a new nature has come to me, I imagine, and I sometimes wonder if I shall ever want to return to peaceful pursuits.

"Surely not so long as these fanatics with their new gods and new religion are devastating the land. They start out and preach and call themselves the Shangti Hwui [Association for Worshipping God], and they gather hundreds and thousands of converts. Their name itself is a treason against the Pure Dynasty, but they would not have been molested if they had not armed themselves and marched for the assault of cities. They burn and pillage, and commit untold crimes against peaceful inhabitants, and force the country people — and those in the towns and cities, too — to go along with them and worship their Tien-fu [Heavenly Father] and the Tien-hiung [Elder Brother, as Jesus Christ was termed by the fanatical Taipings]. But everywhere we have been exterminating these Long-Hairs from the south, and it gives me much pride to know that by my own orders hundreds of their heads have been lopped off.

"When some of the meat butchers at Chi-kiang told me that because of the depredations of these Taipings in all the country roundabout there was no meat anywhere on sale, not even sufficient for a meal, in that city, and asked if some of the Long-Hair prisoners might be killed for food, I told them to see my captain in command over the wretches, and tell him it would do no harm to replenish the meat supply of the city.

."It was the same in Nanking when they were in control. They came in hordes upon the place, and made havoc of the outlying suburbs, and slaughtered right and left. Then, when great breaches were made in the walls, these Long-Haired Rebels poured into the city like floods of fierce devils, cutting and burning and committing all manner of horrible assaults. Their hungry thousands, all the riff-raff and tough characters from that vast region between Canton and the Great River [Yangtse], and far to the westward until Hankow was reached, came in tens of thousands to raise up this new religion and to spread destruction wherever they traversed.

"They had no organisation, although they had great titles and many ceremonies. But their leader, Hung Siu-tsuen, whom they dared to call Tien-teh [heavenly virtue], and his satrap, Yun-Shan, were as wild and unbalanced in mind in all things as they were in religion, and they soon found themselves hemmed in in Nanking — their long tongues sticking out in thirst for water, while their lean stomachs grew as thin as a pig's bladder when it is emptied.

"They would not come out and fight in the country districts along the Great River. No. Neither would they surrender their forces, and accept the leniency of Tseng-kofan, the great soldier and great scholar. No! They would stay only with their large numbers in Nanking until fever swept them away by the boatload, and until the bodies of loyal subjects to the Tseng-chao Throne [Manchu] were killed, so many a day, and the bodies offered for sale in the meat stalls!

"My officers and bannermen have made reports without number to me of the atrocities of the Long-Hairs from the south, and with my own eyes I have been a witness to occurrences that my mother would not believe if she had merely heard tell of them second-hand, or had read of them in books. Yet she, too, and my father have also witnessed the fire and sword of the Long-Hairs; for our own home, the place where I was born, and where at this writing my wife is — for the place has been partially rebuilt — was burned like a stack of rice-straw by the murdering bandits, and hundreds of places in that part were treated in like manner, and the people butchered. Therefore, no orders can be too harsh with such marauders, wild fanatics, who have piled the living and the dead in great mounds, and burned their bodies together. I cannot forgive or overlook their licentiousness and thirst for blood, and I praise all the gods and all the ancestors that I am permitted to be in a position where I may follow them and follow them until they are all dead or driven into the sea."

"*December* 12, 1859. — Report was made to me to-day that P'ing Kli and a brother, both of them friends of mine of student days, were killed in a house-braw on the outskirts of the city. I regretted very much to hear of this affair, though it seems that P'ing, who is half ready to join in the beliefs of the Taipings, poked humour or satire at some of the soldiers, and they hung his body and that of his brother over a bridge. The soldiers' names were reported to me, and I gave orders that they at once be treated in like manner. I do not like to lose good soldiers, especially at this time, but three or four, more or less, will not be noticed much."

"*April* 16, 1860. — My wife has given birth to another boy, and I am happy. I hope he will live to be a great man and a governor-general."

"*June* 16, 1860. — These Wangs [Taiping generals] would murder me as they caused my good and noble brother to die at Taitsang, but there is a plentiful supply of blood in my veins yet, and a brain to accomplish much against the Long-Haired Rebels and their chieftains."

In that same month and year he for the first time mentions by name the "Ever Victorious Army" [The Chang-shing Kiun], of which Colonel Charles Gordon, of the British Army, was later to become commander, and with whom he was to deliver such a succession of telling defeats upon the rebels in the provinces of Chekiang and Kiangsi that the power of the Taipings was completely broken, and the authority of the Manchu Dynasty restored throughout the region. In the mean time the writer of these memoirs, promoted to the command of the Imperial forces in both provinces, was also acting as Governor *ad interim;* and was shortly to be fully commissioned from Peking upon the high recommendation of Governor-General Tseng-kofan.

He writes: "It has never been my belief that it was well to encourage foreigners to meddle in the home affairs of the kingdom, and I believe if I were in supreme authority now, or had been in the years of this Long-Haired rebellion, I would not have memorialised the Throne to allow the English and the French to supply troops in its suppression; but Tseng-kofan is a man of great wisdom, and he is my strongest champion; therefore I will not criticise nor even pretend to follow a path that veers in the slightest from the one he would deem most suitable. Tseng-kofan says the foreigners, at least their religion, is responsible for this present scourge, and that it is well if they lose a few thousand of their soldiers and marines in bringing an end to it. Undoubtedly this is true, but at the same time is n't it possible to believe that these yang kuei [foreign devils] are often at the bottom of such troubles as this, that they may be given a good excuse for stepping in and making claims for their nations on account of their aid?

"Yet, I must say that they have been a great help, more especially the English, who have sent in the past four years many well-trained soldiers to our aid. They are splendid fighters and worthy men, for foreigners, when they are sober; but they have neither liking nor respect for the Imperial troops when they are filled with intoxicants, and it requires much of the time of our patriotic army to keep them within bounds after the capture of a city. They eat and drink everything they can find, but they do not mistreat our women, and they kill non-combatants only upon great provocation.

"I have presented to Wu of Sung-kiang a sum of money to divide with the American, Ward, who is doing such energetic work in recruiting my 'Ever Victorious Army,' and I have recommended to the Viceroy that this man be made a general. I have not seen him as yet, but I have learned of many of his exploits, and am ready to believe that he is a most hard-working and courageous man."

"*January* 5, 1861. — Sung-kiang, which is occupied by the Long-Hairs in great numbers, must be retaken at once at all costs, and I have sent orders to Wu and Ward to consult with me at once regarding it. The 'Ever Victorious Army' has been lying in idleness now for many days, and it may be necessary for me to assume personal command again. I would not care so much about several weeks or months of rest, for I have found that my own body has great pains and fatigue after all this campaigning; but while they are resting they eat more than during this fighting. When they are marching or engaged in battle, they are always on the lookout for food and drink, and they manage to get it somehow. But when they remain idle in big numbers, they get lazy and mutinous, and want the food brought to them. This alone requires the services of many extra men, and the expense of the food is hard to bear. Besides, when they are idle they are given to much excess and lawlessness upon their own accounts, and do not hesitate to demand more pay than is coming to them. I think it is best to keep them fighting; then they are more likely to want to sleep at night, instead of prowling about making trouble for themselves and others."

In December, 1862, we find: —
"It is sad to know that the right kind of a

commander to succeed Ward has not been found, although several have been tried. Ward was an energetic fighter, and if he could only have lived there would be great benefits resulting to the Imperial cause and many honours for himself. In all places where he was in charge he was almost sure of victory, and the Long-Hairs began to fear his name alone.

"I was with him when he died at Tsz'ki, and the tears came to my eyes when he breathed his last. It was affecting to know that he so grieved because he was dying so far from all his family and friends, and this seemed to be of more moment than his actual dying. Though he had drawn in full the pay for all his soldiers, he had a considerable sum due him as lieutenant-commander of the Chang-shing Kiun, but he made no mention of it, and I will have it spent in a shrine to his memory."

The same day he writes: "Neither Burgevine [an American who succeeded to Ward's command] nor Holland [an English ex-officer] has been able to do anything with the reorganisation of the force. I think from their actions they only pretend a military education. I have therefore consented that Major Cooke, who comes with fairly good documents, may take command and see what he can do. Both my feet trouble me, and my back is very lame from last year's fall at Kiang, else I would resume individual command."

"*February* 18, 1863. — I have received word from Sir Frederick Bruce and General Staveley that one of the best of English officers, a Colonel Charles Gordon, will be given us to take command of the 'Ever Victorious Army." The Governor says that this fine officer will serve without pay, which is not only very gracious and generous of the great English Government, but very pleasing to me; for the cost of this long and terrible scourge is appalling to the provincial treasuries, as well as depleting to private funds. Can it be, though, that this officer is not worth much, and that he is of little service to his own Government? In these days valuable services are seldom given unless something of equal or greater worth is expected in return."

"*February* 28, 1863. — Another communication has been brought me from the English, this time from Colonel Gordon himself. He writes but very briefly, in his own language, and says that it must be understood that he is to be in supreme command or not at all.

"That is just the manner of all these foreigners who come into our service, even when they themselves are seeking the position, and are held waiting many days or weeks for their answer. Of course I cannot say this of this English officer, for he did not apply for a generalship nor does he want pay. He does not say this last himself, but his superiors do, and that is sufficient for me. However, if he is an able man and can make of the army the kind of weapon that is needed now to break the necks of all these Taipings, I will see to it — regardless of what his Government may say — that he is well rewarded in honours and money."

(Without date). — "The thought is troubling me that this new British colonel and myself may not get along very well together. That letter of his announcing that only upon the condition that he be given supreme command would he consent to fight the rebels, has caused me considerable uneasiness. Ward said the same thing, so did the useless Burgevine and the incompetent Holland. As for Cooke, he would have been a good general over a crowd of loafers to lead camels to water.

"I hate all these foreigners, but it would not be wise to let them know. It is not the men personally that I dislike, but it is their airs of wonderful superiority. Each and every one sings the same song: 'I will do this and I will do that; I will drive them out or I will kill them all; I'll make your army more glorious than ever; but you must let me have my own way and not interfere with me.'

"That is the whole style of the foreigners, especially as I have seen them in this war. And it makes hair grow stiff on my neck to know that because of the emergencies constantly arising we are obliged to put up with it, and say, 'Yes, yes,' and smile. Some day I will ask them the question: 'Was your country civilised and studying the Seven Arts before ours, and were you born in a century of greater wisdom than myself?'"

Perhaps it might be well here to explain that, without justification, the Taiping hordes which marched upon the defenceless inhabitants of Kiangsi, Anhuei, Chekiang, and Kiangsu, destroying and outraging, and disputing the Imperial authority of Peking, were led by men claiming authority from the "God of the Christians and his Elder Brother, Jesus Christ." This was owing to the fact that their supreme leader, Hung Siu-tsuen, who had at one time imbibed a few dreamy notions from a missionary tract which had fallen into his hands, declared that in a vision the "God of the Christians" had appointed him Emperor of China.

Li Hung Chang, with prominent men of his time, including Tseng-kofan, and Prince Kung, — as well, of course, as the Court, — believed the Taiping Rebellion to be the direct result of foreign teachings in China; when, as a matter of historical fact, the chief Christian missionary of the time in the kingdom, Rev. I. J. Robberts at Canton, refused to take Hung Siu-tsuen's mentality seriously, and made light of the latter's alleged "visions."

In no sense did Siu-tsuen receive encouragement from any Christian nation or quarter, yet the fact of his having announced himself as the anointed one to lead the Chinese people to a religious life such as

the "foreign devils" practised, was sufficient in itself
to characterise the rebellion as a Christian attack
upon the Pure Dynasty, and to place the odium
of the horrible warfare of the Taipings upon the
Church of the foreigners.

It is not surprising, therefore, that Li Hung
Chang, whose relations with foreigners had up to
this time been practically nil, and whose mind had
not perhaps entered upon its broadening period,
should write as we have seen — with more malice in
his heart, no doubt, than he saw fit to commit to
words; yet it is to his everlasting credit that, with
ripening years and a fuller understanding of the
"Western Church," he became, as other parts of
these memoirs tell, one of its warmest friends.

"*March* 27. — It is a direct blessing from Heaven,
I believe, the coming of this British Gordon, whom
I am already designating General. It appears that
he has seen some service before in China with the
Anglo-French troops, and that for a time he was at
Tientsin. However, now that I have met him per-
sonally, and we are quite like friends, I am very well
pleased with him.

"He is superior in manner and bearing to any of
the foreigners I have come into contact with, and
does not show outwardly that conceit which makes
most of them repugnant in my sight. Besides, while
he is possessed of a splendid military bearing, he is
direct and businesslike. Within two hours after his

arrival he was inspecting the troops and giving orders; and I could not but rejoice at the manner in which his commands were obeyed.

"It seems that the British Government simply 'lends' him to us, and that he will not be on the Imperial pay-roll at all. I am afraid that this is bad in a certain sense, for the man that offers his services to you gratuitously is more apt to be independent and ready to throw up his position than the one who is receiving even small wages. I must arrange, some way, to have General Gordon accept money."

"*April* 7. — General Gordon, with 3000 members of the 'Ever Victorious Army' and 15,000 or 16,000 of regular Imperial troops and irregular Provincials, is pressing a hard attack upon the rebels at Fushan. I gave them some pay the day before yesterday and let it be known that as soon as Fushan is completely in our hands another good payment will be made. Then, when Suchau is again under our control, I told them, full payment and a bounty would be given each member of the force under Gordon."

"*May* 2. — A former hein-kwan at Taitsang-fu brought me complaints that Gordon's men, when they captured the place, stripped it as dry as a fish-bone of everything valuable, and killed surrendered rebels by the hundreds. He was very excited, this late hein-kwan, and asked if I would not give him an order to Gordon to protect his life and property.

"The impudence of this rascal, who himself encouraged the Long-Hairs at Taitsang because he
could not hold his office for ever! I long have known
the thieving propensities of this traitor, and, during
the time he was gesticulating his complaint, I was
wondering if it would not be well to call some of the
guard and have an end made to his troubles in the
yard. But I thought better of it, and so sent him
back with a letter to Gordon, written by Hoh in
English, asking the Commander to please cut the
fellow's head off upon its presentation. He went
away very gleefully."

(No date attached; probably written in mid-
May.) — "What a sight for tired eyes and elixir
for a heavy heart it is to see this splendid Englishman fight! I have just returned from nine days and
nights with him, and if there is anything that I
admire nearly as much as the superb scholarship of
Tseng-kofan, it is the military qualities of this fine
officer. Fight — move — fight again — move again
— landing his men — planning by night and executing by day — planning by day and executing by
night! He is a glorious fellow!

"Yesterday when I left him to return for a brief
space, I told him he was my brother; that I considered him worthy to fill the place of the brother who is
departed. Could I have said more in all the words of
the world? The Englishman's face was first filled
with a deep pleasure, and then he seemed to be

thinking of something depressing and sad; for the smile went from his mouth and there were tears in his eyes when he thanked me for what I had said. Can it be that he has, or has had, some great trouble in his life, and that he fights recklessly to forget it, or that death has no terrors for him?"

(Without date.) — "I am sorry there is not entire harmony between Ching and Gordon. The reports from each of them regarding the other indicate an ill-feeling."

"*June* 12. — A number of officers, who have been cashiered by General Gordon, appealed to me to reinstate them, but I have refused to do anything of the kind. It is my belief that they should have been forced away from the army a long time ago. They have no patriotism, but look only for booty and fresh wives."

"*Later. Same date.* — General Ching threatens to resign if some curb is not put upon General Gordon. Perhaps it was a mistake to tell Gordon that he was under my direct orders, and that Ching, though commander of the forces against the rebels, was not to interfere directly with the 'Ever Victorious Army.' Ching is far from being a great military man. Besides, he has a bad temper like Gordon, and they are both quick to say hot words, like myself."

"*July* 19. — Gordon must control his tongue,

even if he lets his mind run loose. To be told that I am secretly favouring Ching and trying to put him in complete control of the forces, including the 'Ever Victorious Army,' when there is no truth in it, and to be further accused of withholding money that is due the troops, is hard to bear. General Gordon demands the respect of those who are inferior to him in rank, and he believes in strong measures to maintain discipline. Why, then, does he not accord me the honours that are due as head of the military and civil authority in these parts?"

"*July* 28. — Ching came again to-day with complaints against Gordon. I drove him from my presence and directed him to return to his command. These things keep me awake nights, and make me sleepy during the hours when I should be devoting my best energy and attention to my duties."

(No date.) — "Gordon thinks of nothing but money these days, and demands coin of me as if I were the god of gold and silver. He says the men will not fight any more unless they are paid. I tell him that as soon as Suchau is in our hands there will be funds sufficient to pay all arrears and some good bounty. This is the word that I have from the Viceroy, and his promises come from the Throne."

During the following week nothing appears in Li's memoirs regarding the numerous troubles and

changes which beset him during that time, culmi-
nating in the virtual resignation of General Gordon
and his departure for Shanghai, where he hoped to
have his action ratified by his British superiors, Sir
Frederick Bruce and General Staveley. But, arriving
in that city, he ascertained that Burgevine, the
American who had succeeded to the command of the
"Ever Victorious Army" upon the death of Ward,
had but lately gone over to the Taipings with about
one hundred foreigners from Shanghai, and was at
that moment within the rebel stronghold of Suchau.
The English officer had for some weeks been making
preparations for an assault upon this city, and, indeed, had reduced and captured Wukiang, Kahpu,
and other important outlying towns and strong
stockades, and but for the jealousies and bickerings
between Governor Li, Ching, and himself, was in
excellent condition for making a successful attack
upon Suchau. He was still very fretful because of
the apparent overlording of those to whom he was
giving his valuable services; but the duplicity of
Burgevine evidently halted the gallant soldier in his
purpose of resigning, and we find him returning to
his post within a few weeks.

"*September* —. — With his many faults, his
pride, his temper, his tongue, and his never-ending
demand for money, Gordon is a noble man, and, in
spite of all I have said to him or about him, I shall
ever think most highly of him. If he would only

scorn to pay any attention to what Ching might say, and forget about the cursed pay for the troops! Damn them! They will do nothing without pay now but eat and drink and sleep; yes, and insult innocent people."

"*September* —. — I have ordered Ching to remain by my side for a time and interfere not at all with General Gordon."

"*September*—. — I gave Gordon a month's pay for seven thousand men to-day, and offered him one thousand taels in English coin for himself. He took it all, saying that he would apply the latter upon the pay of his officers. He is an honest man, but difficult to get along with."

"*November* 28. — The first serious defeat of the 'Ever Victorious Army' occurred last night at the Suchau walls. More than three hundred officers and men were killed and Gordon had a narrow escape. However, he is preparing for a final assault upon the city, and asks me to prevent Ching from interfering with his plans. This I will do."

"*November* 29. — Ching understands that, while he is in command of the Kiangsu forces, he must not attempt to thwart the plans of Gordon in our assault upon Suchau."

"*December 2. Afternoon.* — The Muh Wang [lead-ing Taiping general] was publicly assassinated within the city to-day. It is glorious news, for it shows that the Wangs are not harmonious among themselves, and that our negotiations looking to the surrender of the city will be most welcome shortly. Three thousand women were sent out of the city to-day to be fed by our troops, but Ching drove them back."

"*December* 6. — Negotiations for the surrender of the city being completed, I have issued an order granting pardon to the Wangs and a majority of their followers. The surrender will occur at three o'clock. Gordon is reported as personally visiting in the city. I cannot see what nature of business would call him to go alone to carry on negotiations with the Wangs. Ching has declared time and again that Gordon has a secret understanding with the leaders of the rebels, and even that he has been in communi-cation with the dastardly Burgevine. This does not look right to me, but nevertheless I cannot suspect this man, who returned of his own accord when he heard of Burgevine's perfidy."

In Li Hung Chang's preserved papers relating to this period, but three further references are made to General Gordon, — one in the following brief account of the murder or execution of the Wangs on the night of their surrender of Suchau; and another written on December 29, in which he says that he

offered General Gordon, "on behalf of the Throne,"
a gold medal and ten thousand taels in British coin,
"but he appears injured over the death of the
Wangs, and haughtily refuses the honour and the
gift."

As Viceroy Li, during his famous tour of the world
in 1896, wrote an account of the death of the Wangs,
for the avowed purpose of supplying copies of it to
the English press, in the event that he should be
questioned as to the cause of the disagreement
between Gordon and himself, it is interesting to compare it — as it appears in another part of these
memoirs — with this recital of the affair written on
December 8, 1863, the morning following its occur-
rence, by the Governor of Kiangsu himself: —

"*Suchau. Governor's Temporary Yamen.* — This
is a city of blood to-day, as it has been a vile nest of
rebellion and starvation for so long a time. But in
the midst of it all I am finding a peace of mind and
body such as I have not known for years. A great
and noble victory for the Throne has been won, and
only a few more battles will be necessary to separate
the rotten head of this scourge from its long-decom-
posing body. High credit will come from the Court
for this splendid outcome, and Prince Kung will leap
with joy when he receives the news, which is already
on the way. Gordon and Ching and all the men
deserve high praise; but it is a good time that Gordon's services be dispensed with. He is more head-

strong every hour, and by the way he speaks of the
Wangs one would think that they were brothers of
his.

"Last night, to please the Wangs, I invited them
to a council of peace and a banquet, and it was interesting the way we settled old scores in words. I
spent, too, a large sum upon the foods, and the table
was well set. There was much merriment and good-
nature, and I, too, enjoyed meeting these men —
Long-Haired Rebels though they were. But I made
a serious mistake in not having a strong guard placed
about the east gate, at which my large boat was
lying, and before the banquet was ended a great
horde of lawless fellows, some of them Imperialists,
but a majority of them drunken fellows of the Wangs'
army, poured through the gate, killing and assault-
ing. I was one of the first to hear the great uproar,
and, believing the marauders might be intent upon
dispatching me, — for threats had been made in
many quarters, — I made my escape from the barge
and hurriedly entered the city. Ching also managed
to escape from the hands of the rioters, and followed
me to the landing and into the town. Immediately
I sent orders, by officers we met, to get troops as
soon as possible and arrest all the rioters; but the
orders were not quickly obeyed, and a scene of
wholesale slaughter occurred upon the barge. I
must make report of this to Peking; but it is not
likely that great sorrow will be felt."

"*Same Day. Late.* — Gordon came and accused me of plotting for the murder of the Wangs. I asked him why I should plot, or go around a mountain, when a mere order, written with five strokes of the quill, would have accomplished the same thing. He did not answer. But he insulted me and said he would report my treachery, as he called it, to Shanghai and England. Let him do so; he cannot bring the crazy Wangs back. I am not sorry they are gone, but I regret the manner of their going."

"*Midnight.* — To-morrow twelve hundred of the rebels will be executed. This number will include many of the worst fiends and outragers of the thirty thousand. Some of them, according to my best reports, were engaged in the murder of the Wangs, and they were looking for me."

(Without date.) — "I have received the highest praises from Peking, and Prince Kung says that I may look for a good promotion before many moons. He sends earnest congratulations to Gordon and Ching. To the former I am to offer a gold medal direct from the sacred Throne, and ten thousand taels in English gold."

(Without date.) — "General Gordon called upon me in his angriest mood. He repeated his former speeches about the Wangs. I did not attempt to argue with him, or even to explain the circumstances, as I have done this before. He refused the ten thousand taels, which I had ready for him, and, with an oath, said that he did not want the Throne's medal. This is showing the greatest disrespect, and I shall memorialise the Throne to let him seek other service."

CHAPTER IV

AT THE SHRINE OF LADY YUEN FI

"PEKING, *February 24*, 1873. — Last night, in all the excitement and turmoil of the new order [the Viceroy refers to the assumption of government by the young Emperor T'ung-Chih, of whom he writes interestingly in another part of these memoirs], Her Majesty the Empress Dowager [Tze Hsi] sent for me, and asked with some emotion if I had made any offerings at the temples or shrines, because of the happy outcome of events.

"And I said, bowing lower than the officials then present, though in rank I was above any of that number: —

"'Yes, Most Glorious Empress, at many, but all of them in spirit alone; for, as Your Majesty is aware, I have, ever since my arrival at the Front Gate, been happy to attend to those duties Your Majesty has been gracious enough to honour me with.'

"To this she replied: —

"'Yes, Excellency, these things I know, and, knowing, thank you for. But I will now give you a great command, greater than any man has ever received from his Empress.'

"I waited a long time, bowing low, though not quite prostrate, for I was then privileged in audience without abasement [without lying face downward, prone upon the tapestry of the audience marble]. I wondered if the Illustrious One was to command that of my own personal valour and devotion I was to perform a deed of some darkness. To me, but five nights before the full coming to the Throne of T'ung-Chih, the Empress had intimated a certain wish, the fulfilling of which she might command me.

"Without asking what that desire might be — for secretly I knew it well — I had answered her that my life was hers most gladly, and that the more trying the sacrifice the greater would be my happiness. At that time she had said: 'You are a loyal subject of your word, Excellency, and you have many of them.'

"This quip of Her Majesty's pleased me greatly, for in these times she is not over-humorous even with those whom she most highly regards.

"'Are you of full acquaintance with the Lady Yuen Fi?' Her Majesty asked after long waiting.

"It was unnecessary for the Empress so to question me, and without awaiting a reply she continued:

"'Go between this hour and the same hour not later than two nights hence and make for me a great prayer at the shrine of Yuen Fi. Your Excellency has beautiful words and calm thoughts, even in the times of complexity; and I need not direct you what to say. You may leave the Presence now, but before you do, you may look full upon the form of your Empress.'

"I arose with pleasure in my heart, and it was truly with a great joy that I looked upon the figure of Her Majesty. She had arisen from her seat of Heavenly Grace, and I knew that she was proud of the exquisite attire of yellow silk and yellow gold in which she was arrayed.

"'May I crave a word, Most Illustrious Queen?' I asked, looking into her smiling face.

"She gave assent.

"'My prayer to the Great Lady Yuen Fi will be the holier and more joyful that I have seen Your Majesty arrayed in the garments Her Ladyship invented.'

"My words, I was sure, highly pleased the Empress, and I withdrew.

"Therefore, this night at the hour of the silk-worm, I repaired to the temple of Yuen Fi, and offered up my devotions to that great one in our history, whose art and industry wrought so much for the noble women of our land, and caused the mouths of many millions of people to be filled through the labours they performed.

"I went to the temple with but one secretary of my household and the bearers of my chair, and upon arriving I gave orders at once that the entire place be cleared of worshippers for the space of eighty minutes. Many worshippers had been in attendance at the shrine for several days, for the anniversary time of the taking of the name was at hand."

[Li Hung Chang here intimates, quite asserts,

that the name of China — derived from the ancient Mongol Sin, silk — was selected at a certain known time; but in another place in his writings, "The Domain of the Sin," he confesses that he cannot find authority for any statement of fact in this relation. — *The Editor.*]

"The chief keeper of the temple was abashed and surprised upon hearing my order, which was carried by the household secretary to one of the assistants, and he came and sought me personally outside the entrance.

"'In truth I could not believe it was Your Excellency that had arrived to offer sacrifices to the Great Lady Yuen Fi, and I almost doubted my secretary's words. But if you will have the temple cleared, the while I will give orders to have this done, will Your Excellency be so gracious as to inform his humble servant the reason for this order?'

"'No!' I replied. 'The order is sufficient.'

"With this he went away quickly, after mumbling apologies; but I knew he was not pleased. Instead, I am certain he was much annoyed by my action, for I had heard that in the preceding days he had sought and obtained large numbers of tolls from those who came to lay their gifts and their hearts at the feet of Lady Yuen Fi; and at this hour, as it transpired, he was entertaining with a feast a large number of his family and friends in a part of the temple.

"Whatever his feelings in the matter, it was soon

apparent that the order was being put into effect,
for the worshippers came quickly from the place,
and sought their homes or stood without. Then,
in a time long enough to try one's patience, but sufficiently brief if one had many hours and days to spare
in idleness, this official of the temple returned to
where I still remained outside the entrance, and
informed me that the place was vacant.

"I went to the door and saw that he spoke the
truth. Then I entered, closed the entrance-way
behind me, and went to the sacred shrine of Yuen Fi.

"I remained eighty minutes and ten, alone and
undisturbed, with the spirit of that beautiful Queen
of Industry, to whom I had been sent to speak by the
Empress Dowager. During the eighty minutes I
offered thanks and prayer and praise in behalf of
the Empress, and the remaining time I spoke for
Li Hung Chang; and all I said will ever remain in
my memory, for they were not common words that
I uttered, but heavenly ones borne away to the
heavenly land, where round about the Lady of the
Sin so many who loved her art and her industry,
and were made beautiful or wealthy by it, are her
subjects.

"I returned once again to the palace from the
shrine, but the hour was very late, and I entered only
the Outer Gate, returning then to my own abode."

On the following day this note is found: —
"I am incensed at the action of the chief keeper

of the shrine. Such inquisitiveness in a mere salaried official (one who is known to help himself to gift offerings and tolls as well) is an affront I do not propose to forget. His uncalled-for and impertinent manner did not interfere with my devotions last night, for I represented Her Majesty, and his affront was to me personally, not her. But to-day, when I am preparing a copy of the prayer to send to the Empress, I am hampered in my work by the thoughts of this petty official. Yet the words I uttered are so plain to me that only the mechanical part is made difficult."

"*February* 26. *Hour of the Sheep.* — It is a satisfaction to accomplish things. The keeper Jun came to see me a time ago to beg that his place might not be taken from him. I told him I had nothing to do with his affairs, and did not care to be troubled with small men or matters. He went away with tears in his voice, and will not come back. He should have known better than to come in the first place, for after I had sent in to the Board my word of disapproval of him, he would have to be a very changed man, and a good one, to cause me to seek his reappointment."

"*February* 27. — To-day I had audience with both His Majesty the Emperor and the Empress Dowager. The young Emperor, now a man in years, and, I hope, in the things he may accomplish, is deeply elated when he contemplates his greater growth. I believe that kings, as other individuals, like to feel that the world, which they ofttimes pretend to despise, looks upon them as being past the immature age.

"The Dowager appeared in the lovely dress of three nights ago, when she gave me the unusual mission. This, she explained, was to show me appreciation of the prayer I had uttered on her behalf to the Queen of the Sin, a copy of which, written largely by myself, on silk pages decorated long ago by Fen-lo, was sent her at an early hour for Her Majesty's perusal.

"'You must not claim it as your own; it is too beautiful even for the Metropolitan Viceroy to indite,' she said happily.

"His Majesty smiled, but he did not speak.

"To Her Majesty's words I replied that I could not claim, if I spoke the truth, the prayer to be my own, for it was not. The prayer for eighty minutes was Her Majesty's, I told her; inspired by Her Majesty, coming from Her Majesty's heart and hers alone.

"'But, your most gracious Majesty,' I said, 'the Viceroy, your most abject servant, followed with a prayer of his own for the space of a brief time; and if you will allow I shall beg the sublime privilege of sending you a transcription of my own weak and humble effort. Your Majesty had spoken with such eloquence and flowers of language to the Great Lady

Yuen Fi that my own effort must needs have been a mere school-boy attempt in comparison.'

"'You are loyal and generous, Li Hung Chang,' said the Dowager, 'but send me a copy of your own, for I doubt not it is even as exquisite as mine.'

"Having a copy with me, but written in common characters and upon silvered paper, I presented it with apologies to her.

"But she only glanced at the paper and returned it to me.

"'Your Excellency is too modest,' she said. 'Engross the words on five thicknesses of imperial silk and send them to me.'"

The following is without date, but evidently was written some weeks later at Li's official yamen at Tientsin. The paper was one among a number enclosed in a steel figured box, all of them relating to persons and events associated closely with the proclaiming of the Joint Government, at the Emperor's coming to his majority. The document itself is of heavy silvered paper, badly worn from folding, and soiled from handling, and several lines are missing. It is quite evident that this was the identical paper presented to Tze Hsi, and which she returned to him as an indication of her belief in his over-modesty.

It is interesting to note in this connection that the silver paper manuscript, wholly literary (and religious) in its nature, and in a certain sense chiefly of personal interest to the writer — at least at that time and in the years following — gave evidence of much "thumbing," while a score of documents of considerable political importance were, in some instances, clean and unsoiled.

A HUMBLE MAN'S VOICE

To Thee, O Ancestor of the Silken World,
  a humble man, with face to earth,
  which thou didst bless and make glad,
  asks of thee in all the humility of
  his soul to hear his prayer of praise
  and petition.

To Thee, O Ancestor of a Noble Work,
  it is not given that thou shouldst
  hearken unto my words, for in the
  celestial world of the Seven Springs
  a million millions of them that drew
  from thee on earth the breath of their
  souls and the food of their bodies are
  now thy meekest servants and subjects;
  and the voices of their praise must
  ring so loud and sweet to thine ears
  that these rough words of mine are
  but as jarring sounds of discord.

To Thee, O Gladsome Queen of a Gladsome Art,
  it cannot be known that one so poor
  and miserable as I doth even in thy
  loved land exist, much less that thy most
  degraded petitioner did in all his days
  honour and praise thy name, sing thy glories,
  pray for them that prayed to thee, thought
  by day and dreamed by night of all the
  vast goodness thou didst bestow upon
  this Flowery Land.

But, O Transcendent Lady of the Ancient Sin,
   I, thy miserable petitioner, did, when
   a boy, labour among the trees of the
   mulberry, feed with tender care the
   creatures thou didst teach to spin,
   threaded from their shells the divine
   gleams which thou taughtest to produce,
   wove with mine own hands the silken
   strands of thy invention, and made into
   great widths and breadths the shimmering
   fabric which is the glory of the world.

Yet, O Yuen Fi, Goddess of the Golden Weave,
   all, all the words of this most humble
   man are true; as true as ever lowly one
   did vouch to speak to one exalted high.

And now, Yuen Fi, Lady of the Blessed Silk,
   I crave that thou wilt think of me in
   thy celestial sphere; that to the holy
   ones forgathered there, thou wilt but
   speak a kindly word and say that here
   upon the sordid earth, which thou alone
   didst beautify, there lives a humble man of
   poor renown, who, in all the hours of all
   his days did strive and toil by sweat of face
   and tire of brain to do thy bidding in the
   silken fields; who . . .
           [Lines obliterated]

My prayer, O Heavenly One, O Goddess Rare,
   though I would speak to thee the whole
   night through, in pain I do make brief;
   for well I know that in that High Beyond
   this voice of mine can hold no charm.
   But now again of thee I fain would ask:
   that in this hour of darkest night a
   newer blessing thou wilt give to all that
   work in arts of thine; bless them that

harvest in the fields, bless thou the
silkworms' rounded home, bless them that
toil at factory loom, bless them that mart
thy precious weave, bless them that sail
the far salt seas and take thy goods to
foreign shore; bless them that on their
bodies fair — in Indies and the far beyond,
the lands of Europe and the West, in every
isle, in every clime, in cold and heat, in
shine and rain, in mountain home and valley
mild, in palace rich and humble cot, —
where'er, O Mighty Sun-Loved Queen, thy
name is thought or heard or sung, send
down thy blessings like the dew!

Editor's Special Note. — In three distinct places
in his memoirs, each of them written some years
later when Li Hung Chang was holding the highest
office in the empire, that of Grand Secretary of State
and President of the Council, he makes mention of
the giving of orders by himself for the rich engrossing
and wide distribution of "Her Glorious and Illustrious Majesty's exquisite 'Prayer-Song to the
Goddess Yuen Fi,' to the end that the people everywhere within the realm may not alone learn more of
the great deity of the silk, but that the art and industry which is so dearly beloved of our country may
be encouraged to greater growth and prosperity."

It appears, from an examination of the Book of
Records at the palace, that the Empress Dowager is
credited with the uttering of the "Prayer-Song to
the Goddess Yuen Fi" and its transcription; and it
further appears that inasmuch as Her Majesty was

very jealous of her literary ability — which, *en passant*, all authorities agree was of no mean order — the imperial claim to the authorship of the "Prayer-Song" was never questioned.

It is certain that during his lifetime Li Hung Chang never publicly asserted his authorship of the "Prayer-Song," which he took such pains to order printed and distributed, and to which he refers in one of his published orders as "the immortal words of the greatest of living women to the most glorious and sacred woman of the ancestors."

In the careful examination and translation of the Viceroy's memoirs, including the great mass of public documents, letters, and other papers, no manuscript of a "prayer" or "song," other than the foregoing, was found, although diligent effort was made with that end in view; and while there can be little if any doubt that he was the writer of the "Prayer-Song to the Goddess Yuen Fi," and a copy of it might very appropriately and rightly be reproduced in these pages, yet the fact that it is common enough throughout China, coupled with the inability of the researchers and translators to discover even a duplicate of it among the Viceroy's papers, as well as the further consideration that the "Prayer-Song" rendered into English would cover ten or twelve book pages, make its omission at least a not serious defect.

There is, however, at least to serious literary men in China, as well as in Europe and America, another and far more important consideration, particularly since the "Prayer-Song" is declared by Oriental scholars to be a work of great merit, and as of late years Li Hung Chang has become known as not only a great statesman and diplomat and the richest man of his country, but a writer whose untiring work and high scholarship are bound eventually to give him front rank among the literati of his age.

CHAPTER V

IN THE TIME OF FAMINE

"*November* 30, 1877. — No man in his heart will ever wish for a recurrence of the famine of this year, even though he be a hater of every person in the land except himself. If I live to be twice my present age, I do not expect to wipe out from my sight the terrible pictures of hunger and despair that I have witnessed in so many parts of the north. The Government has not as yet all the facts and figures, but from my own estimates I believe that fully 7,000,000 people have perished for lack of food.

"In such times as these a man wishes that he might be the whole Government, or of such tremendous wealth that he might purchase food for the many who hunger. Even a meal of millet or vegetables every two or three days will keep a man alive, and if he can live long enough succour is bound to come.

"My own purse, during these trying times, I have opened almost as widely as it will bear; but the amount of food purchased thereby is as a handful of grain to a flock of crows. Still, it is a very great satisfaction to know that thousands of hungry stomachs have been at least partially satisfied during these awful months. My men report to me that from one to two thousand are being fed on my corn and vegetables in the city [Tientsin] alone, while I am trying to feed five thousand in the near-by villages. My mother, who has never known want or misery of a like nature in her family, is blessing me every day for this work; and she says the gods as well as the people will not forget that my wealth, such as I have, is not withheld from the poor and needy."

THE SAD SIGHT OF THE HUNGRY

'T WOULD please me, gods, if you would spare
Mine eyes from all this hungry stare
That fills the face and eyes of men
Who search for food o'er hill and glen.

Their eyes are orbs of dullest fire,
As if the flame would mount up higher;
But in the darkness of their glow
We know the fuel 's burning low.

Such looks, O gods, are not from thee!
No, they're the stares of misery!
They speak of hunger's frightful hold
On lips a-dry and stomachs cold.

" Bread, bread!" they cry, these weary men,
With wives and children from the glen!
O, they would toil the live-long day
But for a meal, their lives to stay.

But where is it in all the land?
Unless the gods with gen'rous hand
Send sweetsome rice and strength'ning corn
To these vast crowds to hunger born!

For months the awful famine beast
Has roamed the lands both North and East,
And smiled as he on landscape read
The gruesome figures of the dead.

His black claws clutched the stalwart man,
The very headmen of each clan,
The elder sons and younger ones,
Nor e'en the baby's cradle shuns.

In all the fields along the road,
In each and every mean abode,
He stops to grin in hellish way
At famished forms turned quick to clay.

The greater are the awful pains,
And if the tears do fall as rains,
This monster demon smiles the more
While passing by each hungry door.

He crosses now the bone-dry streams,
And listens to the frantic screams
Of those who on the mountain high
Are doomed this awful death to die.

In valley and on sandy plain
The beast appears, again, again!
In city and in village street,
Where'er you go, the beast you meet!

A million now have bowed to him,
This famine monster, black and grim!
O, gods, we ask, remove the brand
Of this vile demon's bony hand!

CHAPTER VI

DEVOTION TO AGRICULTURE

IN more than twoscore places of his translated memoirs, the Viceroy mentions agriculture as a distinct science to be cared for for its own sake, and, though ever asserting that he is above all things one of the literati, he devotes more space and words to the apotheosis of agriculture than to the glory of literature. Yet this may be satisfactorily explained by these lines, written in his diary at Tientsin in 1879: —

"One of the officers of the Summer Palace of the Royal Blood, who has been reading my high essay on the Divine Husbandman, declares that I must in very heart be more of a tiller of the soil than a literary man; for he told me (without flattery, I believe) that he never had held so high an opinion of the great Shen Nung as when he had finished reading my words. But he went on to say that if I were more devoted to literature I should never have written such a beautiful eulogy; and he wanted to know why I had passed over Mencius and Confucius.

"This caused me to be much amused, and I went on and explained that literature did not need to pay repects to itself; that such a thing would be seemingly selfish, for its highest aim was by the uses of its own beautiful weapons of brain and colours and papers to exalt the other arts and sciences of mankind that were not able thus to speak.

"As we discussed the matter further, I tried to explain that the great philosopher and the great writer reared their own monuments so nobly that any attempts of mine to lift their names would be not only a waste of time, but perhaps would be resented by such persons as would consider me only a minor authority. But with Shen Nung, could I not see his beauties and blessings all about, and yet hear no great voice in praise of him?

"And so he went away satisfied; but not so with me, for he did not give over into my keeping the manuscript he had read with such great pleasure. It was so nicely painted and scrolled (in as many as eight colours, done by my former writers of the Chi-lin family) that I was to have it hung about the walls, piece by piece.

"But I have some other copies, and to-night I shall take joy in reading to the household this piece of mental work, of which I have always been so proud."

It does not appear from the Viceroy's documents just when he composed the Shen Nung Tribute, as he calls it, for several different copies — found at Tientsin as well as at Canton — have different dates attached. One of them, a carefully engrossed copy found at the latter city, bears date of October 12, 1869, or about ten years after his mention of it at

such length as has just been told. This is a careful
version of it: —

MY SHEN NUNG TRIBUTE

(*Written by me from my Proud Heart*)

WHEN I sit down and reflect,
And let my mind and my soul tell me of things so true,
I know that thou,
Most glorious and sublime Shen Nung,
Art the great helper of our people;
The wonderful provider of the world;
The hope of them that have not mines,
Nor great stores, nor forests of hardwood.

But all our wealth comes from thee:
All the funds of our banks,
All the strength of the Government,
All the force of our national progress,
All the muscle of our people,
The beauty of our women,
The hard sinews of the workers,
The strong brain of the banker,
The level head of the statesman,
The shrewdness of the diplomat,
The right arm of the Throne.
(There must always be good blood there.)

We work in the fields:
In the rice,
In the millet,
In the corn,
In the poppy. (The poppy is wrong.)
We work in the vegetables,
In the grain,
And all that is good for man.
But 't is not for their sake alone,
'T is that by bringing them to fruition we raise

A Nation,
A People,
The Middle Kingdom!
And when we do this
We are pleasing the Ancestors.

Shen Nung,
You did not teach us mean arts,
You did not show us the way to cheat our friends,
Our brothers,
Our townsmen,
Our officials,
Even our enemies.
You did not tell us that we should live by sloth,
Nor smart games,
Nor subterfuge.

Therefore,
This day, when I am called to go to the North,
When vast affairs of state speak to me,
When some might think I should be preparing for my
    journey,
I am here saying these things
To Shen Nung.

Even when I was a little boy,
When my father laboured,
When my mother scolded,
When there were mean times in the village,
And I was almost tired of living;
I thought of thee, Shen Nung —
And the green grain thou gavest,
The yellow corn so rich in bread,
The nodding wheat that gives colour to the blood,
The vegetables that give strength to the bone.

You taught us all these things,
You made them ours,
You made them beautiful, and gave them to us.
You bade our land be fertile, the soil in which they grow.

Because you smiled, the winds blew fair,
The sweet rains came like drops of glory,
The sunshine did not hurt,
The moon told the crops to keep growing,
The stars blessed each head of grain,
The dews dropped their blessings
On the corn and the vegetables,
And made them glad,
For the people's sake.
You taught the golden sun to shine,
The night to be cool and refreshing,
The air to be sweet and to soothe,
The trees to hold back the storm,
The grain to bow its heads to meet the blast.

I see in your art,
Shen Nung,
The message of ages,
And ages of sweet thinking.

I see your blessings conceived,
Increased, and multiplied.
I feel the countless hours of thought you have given
To make something
So grand and glorious for the world.

You did not sleep,
You did not rest,
You did not tire,
You did not stop,
Until all this
Was ready to be placed upon the head of man
For his everlasting blessing.

As though you had spun
The finest silk
And hung it there —
A rainbow!

It would appear that at still another time, just previous to a journey to Peking, the Viceroy made a pilgrimage in state to the shrine of the great Patron of Husbandry, for this dissertation is found: —

"In a few days I shall be going north again on a mission of international import; but to-day I could not forbear paying a part of the honours due to ever great and glorious Shen Nung.

"Yesterday I summoned all the persons I desired for the ceremony, and to-day we Tilled the Soil at the Temple. It would seem as if the royalties at Peking thought I would start right away upon the receipt of a message, but to me the Divine Husbandman is more than local or transitory things, for he gave us something that means the good of our people; the good of all the world, I should say, for all time.

"Last year, at this season, I sent a poetic memorial to the Throne, and at the same time wrote an essay which I hope will live along with the works of Mencius. Both of them were dedicated to the Divine Husbandman, and I look for the time when the last one will be read in all the universities of the world. [This probably refers to the Tribute.]

"Some people might think that it was in my official capacity only that I went to-day beyond the East Gate to the temple. Yes, let us agree that it might have been so; for the man in office, especially in high position, is called upon to show good example.

"It is wrong for any man to commit sin with daughters of other men when he has no licence to do so; but it is a grievous wrong for an official to do these things, because he is watched by thousands, and his actions are approved by those who would do likewise. It is this way: When a low man has no right to do a thing (but does it), he is ever ready and willing to cite the example of some individual who is of high estate. He seems to assume that such a one of great office is a kind of god who may be emulated — even when in his own soul he knows that emulation is crime. Great men disagree with each other in such matters, but the common herd only follow like sheep when a man of parts commits folly.

"Again, we know that the low and common herd are for ever saying among themselves: Are there not greater wrongs found among the high than among the low? Do not the mandarins steal more than the boatmen? Are we not for ever hearing of scandals even at the Swan's Lake [probably refers to the Forbidden City], and fewer in the river gutters?

"Thus we know the meaner in mind and in pocket speak of those of exalted position. We know, I say, even though we may not hear with our own ears. For when a viceroy, or a commissioner of the Government, or a mandarin, is met by the kow-tows of the multitude, or when the many may whisper into his ears, if but a word, it is 'Excellency,' 'Your Honour,' or even 'Your Illustrious Majesty!' — fools they are when they use this last to speak to a sub-commissioner of food supply! But they will do it, if but a cash [smallest Chinese coin] is dropped upon the pavements for their dirty hands to grasp.

"And so I say it is for these and other reasons that it is a sign of the highest sagacity for the man in office — the lesser the office the greater is the virtue — to show himself at public functions of patriotic import, to speak strong words for high principles, and at the same time to appear with the greatest outward humility (and inward, if he be sincere) in the presence of noble ancestors or superlative deeds.

"If a coolie decry against the holiness of the Philosophies, he is but cuffed and beaten, or, at most, his wretched head is impaled. Of this there is little or no matter, for even the passer-by doth not enquire the fellow's name.

"But lo! if the governor of a city, the viceroy of a province, doth dare profane! It is not sure that he will be mistreated in his person, nor yet, always, that he may lose his office — for he may have great power in his region. But his words of profanation are as crash of sudden thunder upon the air; the whole city hears the spoken word, and in every house they ask: What was that? And soon it becomes known that the voice was of a mighty man defying something that before was thought mightier. And many of the ignorant, and even those more intelligent, take up the words of the great man, and say one to another: 'Ha! I have thought this way all the time, and now the Governor says the same thing, and I know I am right, for he speaks with great knowledge and high authority.'

"So, thinking over these things many, many years, I know that as I grow higher in the province or kingdom it is the more necessary that by my outward observances I give not only no occasion for scandal-makers or carriers, but that, on the other hand, it is my duty to ever show a respect for the Analects and the Laws, and for every custom that (not called for by the exact privileges of my station) may bring to the minds of the people those things and forms which tend toward a better respect for all the past.

"Yet, as I have said, I go not to the temple of the Divine Tiller for the sake alone of outward observances. Rather do I think that my inward feelings form much the stronger motive: an ardent personal love, combined with a sense of high official duty."

The following lines were written evidently some time later, perhaps after a rereading of the last paragraph, if not the entire composition: —

"How happy indeed should I be if I could speak thus of all my official and private acts!"

CHAPTER VII

AFTERTHOUGHTS OF THE JAPANESE WAR

ALTHOUGH the great Viceroy made many notes in his diary during his sojourn in Japan as Peace Commissioner, even to dictating considerable matter to his secretaries from his sick-bed, — that is, matter of a nature such as is found in his personal manuscripts, for from his sick-chamber he actually continued the carrying on of the peace negotiations, — he appears not to have written much for several weeks after his return to China, where, though acclaimed by the world as one of its most astute and successful diplomatists, he was received almost coldly by the Throne which he had saved from utter humiliation at the hands of the conquerors, and found himself hated and despised by millions of his ignorant countrymen, who charged him with paving the way for the total dismemberment of the nation.

Thus he writes in retrospect at the Vice-Regal Yamen, Tientsin: —

"In one's old age it is terrible to be beset by troubles, worries, and base falsehoods. I should not mind my physical ills at all, at least but very little, if the lies and dissatisfactions which seem to fill the very air could be gathered into a heap and go up in smoke as do the offering papers. Still, there is to me a great personal satisfaction in what I have accomplished, and within my own heart I feel that not in all my days have I had the right more than now to be proud of my labours for China.

"Yesterday, when I returned from Peking, I was sore distressed, for, while I was received by the Sacred Car [Their Majesties] with every indication of a sincere personal liking, there can be no question but that at least they did strongly pretend to be aggrieved over the terms of the treaty. Yet, what would they have me do? — a man with his shoulders flat to the ground, even though those shoulders be broad and strong, does not usually dictate to his adversary terms upon which he shall rise.

"It is time for him boldly to talk terms when he is once more upon his feet! And the wise man — and why not the wise nation? — knows enough to wait until he gets his breath again before talking too loudly.

"If words and gesticulations could win armed battles, the palace and the Tsung Li Yamen would need neither soldiers nor ships. Yet, perhaps, I should not be too severe on Their Majesties nor the Censors, for words won my victories at Shimonoseki. But when a noisy rascal like An Wei-chun memorial-ises the Throne against me — he who could do nothing of value for Tze Hsi in the field nor as a Peace Commissioner, and who has lived by bribery all his days — I am incensed to the core; and were my life younger and a world before me instead of behind me I should take him to task severely. Hound that An Wei-chun is!

"I think that deep within her the Empress understands fully my stand in all this miserable Japanese affair, and that in her own records she will place me right in history. Some men would not care what posterity might say or think of them, but after all these years of mine of ceaseless endeavour, both to help the nation and to build up a name for myself, I cannot bear to think that coming generations might regard me in any light other than a patriot who attempted well and did not always fail.

"From what I am able to learn of my English friends here [Tientsin] nearly all foreigners blame me for the war with Japan. I am not so much interested in what the devils think as in what they say, for, sooner or later, so terribly wide and deep is the devils' influence throughout Asia, that what is thought in London and New York is finally accepted as fact in Hong-Kong, Tokio, and Peking. There is to-day, and has been for nearly a decade, altogether too much correspondence back and forth between our country and Europe. The correspondents write many hundreds of things which are as far from the truth as my life is removed from that of Kang He, or my work in letters from his. And the editors and publishers far away believe all this stuff, — they have no other reliance, because their own foreign offices will not talk, — and so the whole world gets wrong impressions.

"Some say that because I was foremost in advocating an army and navy I should receive the most blame for whatever warlike complications the country gets into. What damnable, hellish, good-for-nothing nonsense!

"The enemies at Peking, getting their tips of thought from some of my enemies abroad, have asserted that because I urged China to make preparations for war — which is as likely to happen to any country at any time as a Yunnan dam is to give way before its flood of waters — I invited the hostility of the foreigners, especially of Japan. Such reasoning is worthy only of a slut puppy! If a bank builds iron doors, or a pawn-shop puts bars upon its windows, may we say that these are invitations to strong-fists and hard-faces to break in? Do we rail at a man, who, having a house full of jade ornaments and rich pottery, causes strong shutters to be placed over his windows so that he may close them at night? If a man stand at the edge of his rice-field, cudgel in hand, while a caravan is passing, do we claim that his attitude is one of invitation to enter and destroy? — or rather do we not commend him as one who is ready to defend his fields that they be not destroyed?

"The truth is, and I have stated it boldly in the north and south, and to Marquis Ito, Prince Ching, and even to the Empress and the Court, to say nothing of the miserable, corrupt An Wei-chun himself, — though I shall never foul my tongue by addressing that hair-brained Censor again, — that for twenty-two years I have been opposed to a belligerent attitude toward our Island Neighbours; and that last year, on the 3d, 7th, and 9th days of the second moon, personally and with vehemence, I urged the Throne against any precipitate action against the Japanese. Upon the last occasion Her Majesty flew into the worst rage in late times, and desired to know if, in matters of international import, I had begun to regard myself as superior to the Emperor.

"Of course I did not, and the question was idle, as are most questions asked or statements made in that condition of mind; and, furthermore, I have been too long a soldier, either giving or receiving orders, not to know what commands are.

"Even one of the first compliments ever paid me by a person of note was when, in Kiangsu, after I had been under him less than two years, Tseng-kofan, with all his knowledge of the academy and the guidance of troops, said that I was not only ever alert to see that orders were obeyed, but promptly and fully to obey in spirit and in letter those which I received.

"Glorious and departed Tseng-kofan!

"My head is very painful to-day. I have written too much and worried too much for an old man, 'an old fool' that damnable Censor calls me — I hope the ancestors hate the culprit — and I must eat and sleep.

"I am afraid this last tea is not so good. Kee

maintains that it is our own best yu-tsin. If it is, I think we had better return to sou-chong.

"An American is here with a letter of Mr. Foster's."

"Hour of the Monkey [3 P.M.]. — I thought the American came with a letter of introduction, and that he might be looking for an interview. I do believe he was a journalist, but he came on a mission that is most pleasing, for he brings a letter from Mr. Foster [formerly American Secretary of State, who assisted Viceroy Li in the Japanese peace negotiations], and he says that all the reports he has been able to receive upon the opinions of men whose views are worth obtaining (in both Japan and the United States) believe that we have come out far ahead in the treaty.

"This is, indeed, news to gladden the gizzard of old Li! I shall see to it that this bountiful harvest of words reaches every part of the country, and particularly the capital. In the south they will learn it afterwards, just as they learn everything."

Secretary's Foster's letter was carefully printed, probably for select distribution by Li, and several copies were found among the latter's papers. While it is not strictly a part of the Viceroy's memoirs, and not in the broader sense confidential, nor even a state document, it is thought justifiable to introduce it in this part of the work.

AMERICAN LEGATION, TOKIO,
June 7, 1895.

MY DEAR FRIEND AND VICEROY, — Your good letter of some two weeks ago has been following me about, and only on Monday night caught up with me here, where I am awaiting Washington mails and further instructions upon certain matters.

I was made happy to hear that your head does not trouble you nearly as much as formerly, and it is my earnest hope that you will be wholly mended by the time you receive this letter. You will recall that one of the last things you said to me was that you would not allow worries to kill you, since the Japanese maniac's bullet could not do it; but I fear you have not been quite true to your word, and that your complete recovery might have been an accomplished fact by this time if you had simply remained indoors, and let nature and the physicians bring you about.

My dear Viceroy, it is the height of folly for you to let your enemies at the capital bother you with their opinions and outbursts. Had you succeeded in annexing Japan they would have accredited you only with ulterior motives.

You must remember, and doubtless you do, that never in the history of the world — so far as I am aware — has there been signed a treaty of peace which pleased all parties, or even one party wholly. One side or the other (more often both sides) is certain that the opposite party got the best of the bargain; and the mission of peace plenipotentiary is at best a thankless one, particularly when you are representing the vanquished, if not the weaker, nation.

It might not be quite politic for me to come out publicly and say so, but I have no hesitation in telling you that all the world, including Japan, outside your own nation, believes you accomplished a truly remarkable victory in the negotiations. My cables from home, some official, but mostly personal, indicate that the Mikado is judged to have lost much that his armies had gained, because of your superior ability; and, between us, we are mutually aware that you did not expect to go home with "a tooth in your mouth or a hair in your head," as you so humorously expressed it.

Therefore, let all this carking, senseless criticism go by. It can do you no harm, either now or in the future. I hear you have lost or will lose some of your decorations and dignities; but they will all come back to you, augmented by others. Whether they do or not, you will be always possessed of the consciousness of having served well your country and people. — Believe me Your Excellency's friend and well-wisher,

JOHN W. FOSTER.

" *Fourth Day of the Sixth Moon* [*June* 30]. — I have seen and heard so many misstatements regarding my actual words and propositions at the Peace Meeting that I am to-day writing the actual pros and cons which led up to the final agreement and signing. This same statement I will send as a supplementary report to the Throne, with the request, which will be granted, that it be inscribed in the Records of the Dynasty. I shall also forward a copy of it to Count Ito, asking that high-minded man to read it and point out to me where I am in error, if I am.

"Let it first be known that only the sincere desire to be of some service to Their Majesties and to the people led me to hazard going to Nippon. I had never set foot on a foreign shore, and it was my wish to live and die in China, without the reproach of setting foot on alien soil.

"At the same time I was opposed to the sending of the former missions. I urged with all my force and strength, first, against the sending of Mr. Detring, and, second, against the going of Chang-yin-hoan, for I could not imagine the Japanese Government, or any other of importance, treating with men of such rank and credentials in a matter of such momentous consequence.

"When I was informed by the Foreign Office that it was determined by the Palace that Chang-yin-hoan be sent, I made haste to protest; for I believed a mission headed by him could result in nothing but failure. Then it was that I was asked, not kindly nor with consideration, if I had been on the alert for such a task myself.

"Why should I be? I had spoken and laboured

against war and, now, if I were to appear anxious
to bring it to an end, it certainly would be charged
that because of personal financial interests, rather
than for the general good, I was hoping to stem the
Japanese advance; for it is as well to put it down in
writing now: no man or set of men in China could
count their individual losses or expenses alongside of
mine. Fen-lo has been figuring for weeks, and he is
still at it, so as yet there is no telling what Li Hung
Chang put into this unfortunate conflict; but in
munitions and supplies (my paid-for goods) about
2,650,000 taels, and in actual cash — the amount
cannot be correctly known for some time yet —
probably 2,300,000 taels. All Peking and Tientsin,
and the centre and south, were aware of this; and
had I rushed forward to urge myself as an ambassador plenipotentiary it would have immediately
been whispered, then talked aloud, and finally told
in the language of lions, that the Viceroy Li, to save
his own private fortune, was willing to sacrifice the
honour of the nation and the glory of the Throne.

"Yes, I wanted peace; wanted it quite as much
if not more than any Chinese, and I was daily and
hourly losing more individually than was any entire
prefecture in the empire, but I was not sufficiently
anxious for it to smirch my name and forever lose
my reputation.

"I had treated with Count Ito on Korean affairs
before, and I learned from agents of mine in Japan
that the Government there wanted to treat with me

in any matters relating to a cessation of hostilities or a permanent peace. This was known, too, at Canton and Hong-Kong, as well as at Peking. The Council knew it, so did the Foreign Office. Still I was not anxious, at any time, on my own account, to go out and seek peace; and it was only upon, first, the entreaty and, finally, the absolute command of Their Majesties that I did go.

"I am not sorry that I went, but my heart is sore distressed to think that my going was necessary.

"It was the Empress herself, for His Majesty, who commanded me to go. For the first time in all my acquaintanceship with Her Glorious and Illustrious Majesty, I had occasion to feel a sense of pity. I had always revered, or, at least, happily and loyally obeyed her; but now it seemed as if the aged Viceroy was her only hope. And I left for Japan with these cruel words ringing in my ears: —

"'You made the war; now see if you can unmake it without humiliating your country before the dogs of Nippon.'

"It was Prince Ching who uttered these words.

"They rang in my tired ears all the way to Japan; they made themselves heard when I met the Mikado's envoys; and they burned into my brain deeper than did the would-be assassin's dirty bullet!

"I wonder if I had died in that foreign land, died in the service of my country, would my enemies have laughed, railed, or shed tears?

"When I arrived in Japan, and the usual formal

courtesies were over with, Count Ito personally
called upon me at my place of temporary abode, and
we chatted as old-time friends rather than peace
ambassadors of two neighbouring nations that were
thirsting for each other's blood. There can be no
question but that the people in north and central
China and the entire people of the Japanese Empire
were feverish for a continuation of the war. What
poor fools the populace at times make of themselves,
more especially when they do not have even a fair
inkling of what is at stake!

"One of the first things Ito said to me was: 'Why
did you send the Kow-hsing to Korea?'

"'I?' I asked. 'I am not the Chinese Government.'

"Thus it was that at the very outset of the
negotiations, the very day of our landing, in fact,
I was made to face the assertion that personally I
was responsible for the war; in other words, that but
for me the Imperial Government would never have
taken aggressive action.

"I made this reply to the chief plenipotentiary
of the Mikado: 'Count Ito, you and I have together
gone over this Korean question before, and we were
able to understand each other perfectly, because we
spoke frankly, and I hope these present negotiations
will be conducted in a similar manner. Therefore,
at the outset, let me take what blame is truly mine.
I did advise the sending of troops to Korea, in fact
many of the troops that came were mine. But I had

the unqualified assurance from Peking that a messenger would leave for Tokio far in advance of any
troopship, and that the Government of the Mikado
would be amply warned of Chinese intentions. In
this, if I was fooled, my province and troops were
fooled, and the nation was brought face to face with
this rupture.'

"'I believe every word Your Excellency is saying,'
said the Count.

"'The Viceroy is unquestionably speaking the
truth, and the truth only,' said Mr. Foster, who was
with me when Count Ito called.

"There was a silence of many moments following
these words of the American diplomat, and during
that time I noticed that there were friendly and
knowing nods between the latter and the Japanese
ambassador.

"'As to the Kow-hsing, Count Ito,' I said — 'if
this is simply an informal talk between us, and not
to be carried into our negotiations — I think your
treatment of our ship was abominable and barba-
rous.'

"Ito made no comment, though his face twitched.
I believe he fought hard in order to keep back that
word 'Yes,' which was struggling within him.

"Shortly after this he took his leave, and we did
not meet again until the opening of the formal conference next morning. Mr. Foster remained with
me a large part of the day and well into the night;
and here is a fitting place to say that I feel that

China should ever remember him as a great national
friend, just as I shall ever cherish him as a true and
helpful personal one. Indeed, I do not hesitate to
say that but for Mr. Foster the case might have
gone more heavily against us, though he was by no
means one-sided in his views — on several points in
the dispute actually taking the view of the Japanese.

"My very first proposition to the conference was
that an immediate armistice be declared. I urged
that inasmuch as we, the fully accredited representatives of our respective nations, were there assembled
for the avowed purpose of arranging a peace protocol,
it was extremely strange if the very Governments
which had sent us upon our missions should at the
same moment and hour be issuing orders to generals
in the field and admirals on the sea.

"I spoke for some time upon this phase, one of
the longest addresses of the kind I ever made; and
when I had finished there was silence for many
minutes. This was followed by the retiring of Count
Ito and his colleagues to a part of the room by themselves; after which they took their places, and
Count Ito said: —

"'Your Excellency's proposal is agreeable to us as
representatives of Mutsuhito, His Imperial Japanese Majesty; but we are compelled to demand that
during at least the period of the armistice the Chinese
Government shall turn over for safe keeping the
fortress and munitions, permanent, at Taku and
Shanghaikwan, the railway and rolling stock of the

Tientsin line, free of every interference, and the fort and munitions, permanent, at the city of Tientsin.'

"I was dumbfounded at this proposal, and had I not kept fully in view the great seriousness of our conference, and the nature of the men composing the Japanese delegation, I should have thought Count Ito guilty of perpetrating a great bit of humour. Frankly, I was astounded to think that such a condition — precedent to an armistice — should be made, and it appeared as if I were unable to find words with which to express my surprise. Indeed, all I could do upon the moment was to ask Count Ito to have the graciousness to repeat what he had said. To think that he seriously intended that we should turn over the Gate to the Capital itself, together with our munitions of war, was truly baffling.

"Count Ito repeated, word for word, as before.

"As he proceeded each syllable seemed to rouse a new anger within me, and it was with considerable difficulty that I restrained myself when he had finished.

"I looked over at Mr. Foster, who was only as a spectator up to this time, and I saw that his face was ashen.

"'Are those your best and only terms?' I asked as calmly as I could of the Mikado's chief ambassador.

"'They are the only terms for an armistice,' he replied.

"'Then let the war go on while we talk peace,' I answered.

"And the first session of the conference came abruptly to a close."

"When I was again in my abode and alone, I went over the situation phase by phase and step by step, and reluctantly I came to the conclusion that the Japanese Government meant to impose about the hardest conditions possible to any terms of peace. The Japanese were as fully aware as myself of the conditions in China, for, for years, to my certain and personal knowledge, they had had spies, emissaries, and agents from one end of the country to the other. Peking, Tientsin, and Nanking were fairly alive with Japanese civil and military officers, some of them employed at the hotels, some on estates, many of them in the foreign concessions, and a few, as I learned, even drawing salaries or stipends from myself. Of course, when I learned of these latter they were forthwith put out of harm's way.

"But China was wholly unprepared for a conflict with Japan, and it is with no sense of personal boasting that I say that no one knew this terrible fact better than myself. Yet I had been in favour always of maintaining our position in Korea, for that country had been for centuries the vassal of China; and had she not been a lone long peninsula running down in isolation from Manchuria, the Japanese would never have deemed themselves as possessed of any more rights there than in Shantung, or my native Anhuei. But for the sake of peace with her neighbour China had agreed, in the Convention of 1884, at Tientsin, when Count Ito also represented his country, that both our nations should withdraw their troops from the country, and allow the King of Korea to look after all internal disturbances of that realm. And it was further agreed, to this solemn effect: 'That in case of any grave disturbance occurring within the kingdom of Korea, of great moment or concern to China or Japan, such as might of necessity call for troops from the outside for the suppression thereof, it is hereby understood and agreed that they shall give, each to the other, previous notice in writing of their intention to send a force; and that after the matter which made the call for such troops necessary is settled, such troops shall forthwith be withdrawn, and other troops shall not be further stationed at any place or point within the recognised kingdom of Korea.'

"It was claimed by Japan that the Chinese Government broke this solemn clause. If it did so I myself was misled, for, as I informed Count Ito, and as I have already written, I was given plainly to understand at Peking that proper notification had been sent to Tokio a reasonable time in advance of the sending of help in response to the call of the Seoul authorities. The King believed himself unable to cope with the wild Tong Hak, and he very rightly asked the Throne for assistance, just as his country had been doing for centuries.

"I have made this declaration once before in the presence of the high contracting parties of the two empires, and with Mr. Foster a witness; but I wish here to record it as my eternal judgment.

"Had not the Japanese Government been determined to possess Korea at any cost, some time or another, it would not have hastened to despatch an army corps to that country immediately — immediately, I repeat — upon receiving the bare information that Chinese troops had gone to Seoul in response to the appeal of the King of Korea. China did not force her troops upon Korea, nor did she seek for an opportunity nor an excuse to do so. On the contrary, the Throne and Government were quite willing, even anxious, that Korea attend to her own affairs. That country had long been a considerable burden upon China, and while there was, and is, and always will be, the kindliest and most sympathetic bonds between the Hermit Kingdom, so called, and the Chinese Empire, the latter country had nothing to gain even by substantially and politically incorporating Korea as a province to be governed from a vice-regal yamen in Seoul or more directly from the Northern Capital.

"Had Japan not been anxious to force a war upon China, the Government of that country would never have countenanced, before nor afterward, the sinking of the Kow-hsing, and the consequent murder of hundreds of brave men who not only were in a defenceless position themselves, but were going in obedience to orders to assist in the pacification of Korea — not in any attack upon Japan.

"I charge that the Government of the Mikado deliberately sought a conflict with China for the sole purpose of annexing the so-called kingdom of Korea. I charge that the methods pursued by the Japanese were underhanded and uncivilised. I charge that the destruction of the Kow-hsing was deliberate and wholesale murder, perpetrated in the name of a Government that pretends not only to be a leader in Oriental thought and learning, but to have absorbed the best of Occidental ideas and principles.

"These are my own personal feelings and statements, but they are susceptible of corroboration by general facts of this war, and by records to be found in Tokio and Peking. Perhaps some will say — people say everything and anything when my life and motives are under consideration — that it is my duty to gather these proofs and submit them for the judgment of the world. Some will say that I owe this duty to China, if not to myself. Some will denounce me if I do not follow such a course. I should be denounced and vilified in any event.

"But I have great and potent reasons for maintaining silence at this time, and I am sure that every statesman in the world will agree with me.

"I have lately returned from a peace conference. The awards and the settlements have been made. The war is at an end, and peaceful pursuits are again occupying the attention of the people. My name has been signed to a great document agreeing that our troubles are things of the past, and that each nation now looks to the other for friendship and right dealing. My country feels her humiliation, and personally I am in disgrace.

"Looking upon these things and giving them careful thought, who is there, Government or people, at home or in foreign lands, that would forgive me if I were to open up all the old cuts again and precipitate a renewal of the strife? Such I am sure would be the result if I were to speak out to all China and to all the world as I have spoken man to man, to Count Ito at Shimonoseki. And I am not writing these words with any thought that they will be given publicity within a period during which any of the hot animosities engendered by this deplorable and uncalled-for conflict may remain. I hope for peace for China, peace for Japan."

One week later at Peking the Viceroy wrote: —

"I have pored over a mass of translated correspondence from St. Petersburg to-day, part of which is from my friend Count Cassini, and my old frame seems to be given thereby a new elixir of life! I can return south with better feelings, if less honours.

"Now once more the Throne feels more friendly, but there is an apparent coldness in the treatment accorded me by the Empress. Yet she was gracious enough to acknowledge that the satisfactory assurances are the result of my representations to the

Russian Court, last year, when these troublous times were approaching.

"The Empress is a strange woman, contradictory, and headstrong as the devil at times; but if she feels she has done a great wrong, she is ever ready to right it if her personal dignity is not too plainly at stake.

"Yesterday her mood was that of desiring me to say things in my own behalf. She had learned within an hour of their arrival the good tidings from St. Petersburg, the gist of them; and I was admitted to her presence shortly after.

"Briefly we discussed the Russian letters, and Their Majesties are heartily grateful that Japan will not be permitted, either now or in the future, to seize upon any part of Manchuria or the mainland.

"Why did I not have these assurances before I went to Japan?

"Had I known the way the Czar's Government feels in the matter of Japanese aggressions in Korea and in Manchuria, after my armistice proposal had been answered in the manner it was, I could have said — and would have said — to Ito: 'Go ahead with the war!'

"Still, there is often a very serious doubt in my mind as to the real object of these Europeans, and I have found that some of their most able and honourable diplomats will lie with as much ease as a Nanking bird-hawker. They will be as extravagant in their promises as a man who wishes to borrow

money but who also has no security to give —
especially England; they swear they intend to do
one thing, and it is certain that beforehand they had
it all figured out how they would do another.

"Russia is to-day our greatest friend and our
most-to-be-feared enemy. She is our friend because
Great Britain and France pose as friends also. She
wishes to be a better friend than they. She is our
greatest enemy, because what the Russians call the
trend of her destiny makes her so. She dominates all
northern Asia, and hopes some day to have prepon-
derating influence in China.

"She will help us to keep Japan out, because she
herself wants to get in."

"*July* 28. — I cannot think that all people are
bad, even the worst of the Christians, for to-day
I had an experience — just an hour ago — that
makes me think that outside of office and business,
outside of riches and honours, there are small hap-
penings which touch a man's heart, and make him
feel that humanity is not all iron and gain and falsehood.

"For to-day this yamen, which for twenty-four
years had been mine, was the destination of a great
mission, such as never came within the compound
before. I nearly wept to receive them.

"Two native Christians all the way from that
miserable town in Japan to bring me here medicines
for my head, and to see if I was getting better! I

wonder if this is because Christianity teaches such things? It must be, for the Japanese are a race that assume to be strong in matters of physical pain, and they are a people that hate the outsider — the Chinese most of all. Therefore, it must be some new ideas that this man and boy got into their heads to make them do such a thing.

"With my own eyes I saw them coming up the steps of the yamen, and at first I told Len to send them away — as if I were proprietor of the place; but I soon saw that they were Japanese, and I wondered what they might want of me, or if it was I they desired to see. Len let them in, but for a long time we could not learn just what was desired; for the man spoke his own tongue, or a dialect of it, and I could gather but a few words.

"Ling-ho, one of my interpreters, being sent for, I was amazed to learn that the strange man was one of a number of native converts who had called to see me in my sick-room when I was recovering from the effects of the madman's bullet in my skull; and as I looked at him I saw that he was telling the truth, for I recognised him. His name, he said, was Sato, and the boy that accompanied him was his thirteen-year-old son.

"Sato said that all the native Christians in the little mission at Ketuki, near Moji — the mission that had at first sent the delegation to my sick-room with flowers — had talked about me every day since I was there, and had prayed to the Christian God for my recovery. He said that they, his mission friends, did not believe in war or killing, and that they had understood that I had come to put a stop to the war.

"'Were we not right, Your Excellency?' he asked.

"'Yes, Mr. Sato,' I said, 'you were right. I went to try and stop the war. There has n't been any since, has there?'"

"He answered no, and said that I was a great and good man.

"Then he explained that all his friends were very anxious to know how I was getting along. Sometimes, he said, they would hear that I was entirely well, and again it would be reported that I was dead; so they could n't stand the uncertainty any longer, and collected money between them and sent Sato with a message of good will and some herb medicines.

"I took the medicines and had my two visitors served with the nicest kind of boiled chicken, some chicken tongue on crackers, rice, cakes, and tea. I wanted them to stay with me for a few days, telling them that I would treat them well; but Mr. Sato said he was already almost sick unto death to get back home, and that he had once or twice nearly turned back, especially as his son was so lonely. Besides, he said, he had been driven almost to distraction, not knowing whether he should find me here, at Peking, or in the south.

"When they were ready to go I gave them a big

bundle of presents of all kinds for their friends back at Ketuki, two hundred taels for the mission, and as much more to reimburse them for the outlay of the journey. This last he did not want to accept, saying that as he had funds sufficient to take him home he was fearful that the friends who had sent him might not like it. But I prevailed upon him to take the money.

"I think this Christianity makes poor and lowly people bold and unafraid, for before Mr. Sato and his boy left he wanted to know if they might pray for me. I said they could, expecting that he meant when they got back home again; but he said something to the little son, and they knelt right there at the door and said a prayer. I could not keep my heart from thumping in my bosom as I watched that poor man and his frightened little boy praying to God — the God that will deal, with me and with them and all mankind — that I might be well of my injuries.

"I was sorry to see them go.

"In this old yamen, which for twenty odd years was mine, strange scenes have been enacted, great councils held, and midnight conferences affecting the whole world have taken place. I have received royalties and dukes, ambassadors, ministers, murderers, robbers, and beggars. Men have been sentenced to death from here, others have been made glad with leases of lands, railroad contracts, or the gift of public office. But during each and every oc-

currence, whatever its nature, I have been complete
master of my house and myself — until an hour ago.
Then it was that for the first time did I believe the
favour was being conferred upon me."

Li was not "master" of the yamen at this writing,
simply making it his headquarters during his stay
in Tientsin.

"Poor, good Mr. Sato, all the way from Japan to
offer a Christian prayer for the 'heathen' old Viceroy! I did not know that any one outside my own
family cared enough about me for such a thing.

"I do not love the Japanese, but perhaps Christianity would help them!"

CHAPTER VIII

A COUP D'ÉTAT ON THE HORIZON

THE first intimation in Li's memoirs that he anticipates serious trouble for the country through the machinations of what he terms the "reformers" and "reactionaries" occurs in the following lines, which, though accompanied by indication neither of place nor date, were probably written at Nanking in early May of 1898, because treating in the first part of the death of Prince Kung, which occurred on May 3 of that year: —

"Not in many months have I heard news that is so disheartening as that which came yesterday and is confirmed to-day. All night long I had repeated petitions to our ancestors that it might not be true; but Heaven sent for Prince Kung, my old and tried friend, who has been a fighter in the political and other arenas for nearly forty years, and who in influence during all that time has been as a water level for rash and hasty ones in the Government.

"The Prince has been a true patriot, and the country will miss him. If he had died ten years ago, or even just following the Japanese troubles, the blow to order and moderation would not have been so severe; but his going now, to be a guest on High, when China needs all the balance she can secure, when a ferment like the very yeast of hell is working

in every part of the body politic, and when a lot
of crazy-brained zealots and bigots have the ear of
the Throne, if not the arm, his strong mind and fear-
less voice is needed at Peking.

"It would seem that a great many people do not
imagine they are doing things at all unless they are
going to extremes. From the cold of the Calgan
snows they rush to the heats of India or the other
way about. It is either murder with them or a
sickening honey kindness. They want to yell at the
top of their voices from a temple pagoda, or go down
to a deep well and whisper at the bottom. Some
brains are so constituted, or mixed, that if a thing
does not appear white to their mental vision it is
black, if it is n't yellow it is green, if not red it is
blue. They take no bath at all, or they scrub their
bodies until no skin is left. They will eat like hogs
and just so often, or they go fasting, and scorn a
chicken's tongue or a thin cracker.

"It is just so with too many of our public men.
They are like acrobats that jump from one side of
the stage to another, just to let people see that it can
be done.

"Oh, but Prince Kung was not one of these, and
it grieves me more than I like to confess that he has
been removed by the gods from the place in life he
so well filled, and wherein at present he is so direly
needed. If I could bring him back I would turn over,
for the nation's sake, more than one half of what I
own; even though Kung himself never helped me

to accumulate a dollar, but rather put himself in my way two or three times.

"But, after all, what is wealth? My noble and severe parent had it in goodly quantity, but it cannot be said that it made him happy. He was far from being a happy man. I suppose that when he was the husband of one wife he thought he would be happy with two; but when the second was there, it appeared his idea of happiness called for another. I am glad that it did — but this has nothing to do with the argument — for that third and lesser wife was my own good and mild mother, who scolded only when it was absolutely necessary, and who raised a son to my father who has been able by his own exertions to lift himself above all the other children, and at the same time 'put rice in their pockets and hams over their shoulders' [i.e., to assist to wealth and office].

"And so it is with many people. I remember when I was a youth at Lou-Chow that riches and promotions seemed as very gifts of the Celestial Regions. But I have found that neither great wealth nor distinguished decorations, nor both put together, will guarantee a man against unrest of mind or turmoil of soul. How great and honourable is the Peacock's Feather of the Throne, yet how much easier rests the head on goose feathers!

"Therefore would I give about all I possess in worldly goods if Prince Kung could be spared to China another year or two. I am getting old, almost beyond the years of strength, and I fear that unless supported strongly I cannot withstand a long battle against the hurly-burly, hit-or-miss crowd, able to see little beyond its own compounds.

"Prince Kung and myself, in the French crisis of 1881, stood together, shoulder to shoulder, voice to voice; and from that day to the present — this is sad to think that he is silenced — we have laboured for the safety of our country, and have saved her from being sliced like a watermelon.

"Reformers! reformers! — idiots and liars, and enemies of their country, I call them!

"Under the guise of reform, they, led by one who is close to the Emperor, would turn things topsy-turvy in a month, and build a nation over again. K'ang Yuwei is a good man in himself, and deserves his doctorate of letters — I admire his writings and his speech very much — but he does not seem to realise that in advocating wholesale reforms, even though he do so with the best of motives, he is simply affording a different class of 'reformers' — crazy, hunchbacked barbarians — opportunity to carry on this propaganda against the foreigners. K'ang Yuwei, because of his learning, his brilliancy, and his earnestness, has the Emperor under his thumb, and he is holding him there until the other 'reformers' (who laugh over their moon shoulders at both) have the fanatics aroused to do injury to the foreigners, and thereby bring upon our heads the maledictions of the Powers."

"*May* 30, 1898. — I am too ill to go to Peking, though I feel that what weight I may exert to offset K'ang Yuwei's influence at Court is sorely needed. It was regrettable that I could not attend the funeral of dear Prince Kung."

"*June* 6. — My health is somewhat better, but I fear the country is becoming ill."

"*June* 7. — To-day, even in the sadness of my soul, I have attended to much correspondence. I took occasion to write K'ang Yuwei, warning him that he was leading the Emperor too rapidly through forests neither of them had traversed before. My letter will anger them, and I shall receive, if anything, a most spirited retort from the Emperor's tutor. Nevertheless, I would write just such a letter every day, and knock, if vainly, for admittance to the audience room, if I thought the mad trend of affairs could be stayed."

"*June* 8. — The Emperor, led on by a few first notions of reform, would turn water into rice, wine and sand into fine meal. K'ang, with the best of intentions, appears to have lost his balance, and of course the Emperor is unbalanced with him. They probably do not realise that their own childlike upsetting of things simply gives a cover under which the anti-foreign agitators may continue their suicidal propaganda. Only to-day I received by a courier, without knowing who sent it, or why it should have been sent to me above all others, a vermilion placard which reads: 'The Throne is instituting wholesale reforms. Let all patriots band together that the foreign devils may be driven out of the country, so that the people of the kingdom may enjoy the gracious and beneficial reforms the Emperor may provide.'

"I hear that Mong of the Board of Rites has rashly attempted to memorialise the Throne against some of the Board and one or two of the Censors. Poor fool, he is taking the Emperor at his word, and thinks that he is already in the latter's confidence."

"*June* 17. — I am leaving for Peking to-night, determined to see Tze Hsi herself, and present the situation to her in the plainest manner, just as I see it."

"*Tientsin* [without date]. — It was told me since my arrival here — people do not care what they say to a man when he is ill — that 'all the patriots' are regarding me as a reactionary, while I formerly posed as a reformer.

"If these very forward and intelligent persons would define the words as I do they would find that they have been changed about. I think that it is possible for me to say with truth and pride that for twenty-five years I have been the champion of true reform throughout the empire; but I do not believe in tearing down one's house in order to build a new one which is to have a gable which the other lacked. I think if a man wants a gable or another window or a door to his yamen, he should go right ahead and make the alterations; but a man is insane who will tear down his entire length of wall in order to change the place of entrance to his yard. Why not kill all of your flock of turkeys because one of them has a limpy foot?

"K'ang proposes to cure all the ills of the nation by one great dose of reform medicine. He would have the Emperor building his own fires, and the ladies of the household washing their own linen. He thinks the Board of Mines and Railways will in a week or a month solve problems, and do away with prejudices that have occupied the attention of this country for two thousand years. He believes that every man with a grievance should have the right to memorialise the Throne, and tell his difficulties into ears that are already burdened with such things.

"K'ang Yuwei, you are an excellent educator, your writings are elegant, and better speech than yours is not heard in all the Middle Kingdom, nor beyond; but you are making an ass of the young Emperor, and it is only a question of time when Tze Hsi will make a bigger ass of you! . . . I am sorry that this is so, for your sake; but I am more sorrowful still for the sake of the country, and within the next few hours I am going to speak these words to your face: —

"'You are a reformer; yes, a reformer who will make a back handspring into a worse mess than you are trying now to get out of. I would not say these words to the Emperor — he's too inexperienced to know that they are true, and too light-headed to believe them if he knew. Nor will I speak against you to the Dowager Empress. But if I were the ruler of China to-day I would send you back to teach a lot of undergraduates their letters, or I would part your head from your shoulders!

"'Remember, Honourable K'ang, chief tutor to His Majesty, I give you credit for a patriotic heart at the same time that I tell you your brain is a muddy mill-pond called reform, in which older and stronger men cannot see a decent fish. You love your country, but you would make a fool of her; just as the lovesick rustic, rattle-brained over his new toy, would make her forever ashamed by embracing her in the market-place.'

"Being called to the palace now for consultation, I shall make an effort, according to my duty as I see it, to put a damper upon some of these alleged 'reforms.'

"A reform that means going backward is laughable when it is not tragic.

"A reform that tears everything down before attempting to build up is a hurricane.

"A reform that assumes that the whole world went bad in a week, and that it can be made good in a day, is a senseless thing. .

"I hate a professional reformer as I hate a nagging woman; each has the idea that the other party was not endowed with even a place for brains, to say nothing of possessing any mentality.

"But in my very soul I feel that the wild new-doings of the Emperor have given tremendous encouragement to the anti-foreign sentiment; and that once again, but without the strong power for suppression which was mine in the days of 1870 and onward, when I put an end to the killings and wrong-doings in Pe-chili, I am called upon to do my utmost in the cause of internal order, that the excesses of the country may not bring the outside Governments within our gates again."

"*At the house of the late Prince Kung. July 9. Hour of the Dog.* — Since my last arrival at the capital, I have scarcely put in an hour alone. In truth no period of my life, of equal length of time, has been so filled with work that should have accomplished much but which, I fear, really amounts to so little. It is too bad I am not an ignorant man owning a single dromedary. Then I would crawl close to my beast on the roadside, or in his stable, and sleep in peace until morning; but youthful ambitions and forty years of unceasing labours have brought me an old age of turmoil and upheaval, and I shall not shirk my responsibilities, even though the tired blood be spilled upon the ground through the great artery of my neck!".

"*Home Place, July* 11. — For more than two hours after midnight I was at the Empress Dowager's own palace, and for more than one-half of that time I was in secret audience with that woman who has often said that twenty minutes was sufficient time for her in which to give orders and answers to the Council, the Cabinet, and the Foreign Office combined.

"It was a bad omen that the Dowager held in her hand a communication from Kang-i, and that Tung Fuh-sing had been in audience with Her Majesty thrice during the day. Fuh-sing, too, claims to be a 'reformer,' but his idea is to 'reform' the finances, 'reform' the Emperor, and 'reform' the Christians. He has Kang-i with him, or rather is with Kang-i, and together their influence over Tze Hsi is indeed deplorable — quite as bad, except in a different direction and for different ends as K'ang's crazy dominance of His Majesty. Yet one begets the other, for the more foolish the Emperor becomes under the tutorship of K'ang — curse his snake hide, why does he not teach only things of which he is competent? — the more rabid becomes Her Majesty under the evil eye of Kang-i, Tung, and Prince Tuan. If she would but listen to the wise counsels of Prince Ching and Jung-lu, her manner toward all the world would soften, and her ending years would be those of peace and comfort such as she fully deserves.

"I believe with the flight of time her ambition grows, and she hopes to live on for ever. Poor

Empress! — she does not understand that these constant bickerings, midnight counsels, and harsh words are making her life as bitter as aloe juice and iron mixed with rain water.

"To me Her Majesty put the question direct, as to where I should be found in the event of a great trouble.

"'Just as always, Your Illustrious Majesty,' I replied.

"'And where is that?' she questioned further.

"'A million pardons, but does Your Majesty need an answer to that question?'

"She was apparently impatient with my seemingly evasive answer, but she did not look angrily upon me as is her custom when offended ever so slightly.

"'But I wish to know!' she commanded.

"Then I told her that I should be found always with her and China, just as I had been all my days.

"'My days, Your Majesty,' I said, 'are not many; but such as they are, you may count upon your old Grand Secretary.'

"'In any event?' she persisted.

"'In any and all events,' I answered.

"Then she indicated that the present audience was at an end, but as I had remained about the palace until two o'clock in the morning, and as I hoped she would not find it necessary to summon me again to-morrow night, which she had intimated might be the case, I did not immediately retire; but urged that if there was a premonition of trouble in her mind, and if she reposed in me the trust I hoped and believed she did, would it not please her to put me at greater ease regarding her plans?

"She had been so cordial and amiable in comparison to her ordinary wont that I did not believe my further query would offend her, but in an instant she was alive with wrath and angry words, and I immediately withdrew.

"I have seen women something like her before, but they were in my house, and it was not necessary for me to get down on my knees to them."

"*August* [no date]. — If my counsel amounts to anything in the affairs of this nation, I am unable to see in which direction or quarter, for I find myself utterly opposed to the desires and policies of either one of the factions that seem bound to bring about a great social upheaval, if nothing more.

"The Emperor — less of a monarch than my youngest son — is inaccessible to friend or foe, and I am beginning to feel that his end is near. But really I should have no pity; nor have I, as a matter of fact; for, under the spell of those feather-minded ones about him, he refused to listen, even listen, to certain words of wisdom I would have uttered. With his eyes wide open like a frightened feline, he still was so blind to all truth and all manifestations of events that the Palace of Heaven itself would be but a mere speck upon his vision.

"The One-Thought K'ang has gone. What a pity a year ago did not see him back with his classes!"

[Without date.] — "It is as I thought regarding K'ang. I did not believe he had even sufficient reason or wisdom to perceive the avalanche that he was bringing about his own head with the great reform wind he himself stirred up. He is gone from Peking, and I trust he has not failed to perform that act which would fittingly crown his work of the past few years. I have no personal animosity toward Yuwei, nor his memory; but I hope he has taken himself to other spheres, where he may be of some use to K'ang and those about him. I wish his memory well, and if I knew for certain he was dead I would make an offering this very hour."

[Without date.] — "Personally and with my own hand — for Fen-lo is no longer with me, and I have found few others to have any confidence in — I have sent brief letters to my friends in the foreign legations, telling them of the events which they may soon expect. If some of those who always enjoy picking at the bones of the old man knew this, they would be avowing that great national secrets were being divulged to the foreign devils.

"I know affairs are going to be bad again, and perhaps there will be a season of massacre and burning. But what can I do? I have exhausted every reasonable resource in speech and writing, and through the influence of such friends of mine as still may have an opportunity for a hearing at Court; but I fear it is all unavailing.

"Jung-lu sent me a lengthy communication to-day. He does not say as much, but I am sure from the tone of his splendid letter that he feels that a reactionary movement of the most momentous kind is contemplated by Her Majesty. Jung-lu knows.

"He asks me to send word to my friends in the different Governments not to be alarmed at any event that may follow in the next five or six weeks. This is just what I have already done. We do not want the Powers to think that in any emergency we have been taken by surprise, or that widespread outrages upon native Christians or missionaries will necessarily follow. It is true that we fear these very things; but the coming of foreign troops would only increase the tension at this time, and perhaps be the very means of precipitating a vast outbreak.

"Her Majesty itches for the name of being Ruler. She is not satisfied with the amount of glory that has been and is hers, and her mind has been very fully poisoned of late against all things foreign or Christian. The best that we can do — we who are still friends of hers (though some of us are held at a great distance) — is to keep our peace as best we may, and not too strongly oppose the radical hotheads who are apparently completely in the ascendancy at the palace. Her Majesty would not permit a physical injury to be done even to the end of one

of my toe-nails, though I might openly oppose her
in the scheme she has on foot; but, for the sake of
the greater good in the end, I must appear to be in
accord. What does it avail a man to whistle in the
teeth of a gale, or cast a jug of water against a tidal
wave?

"Apparently, for once in my life, I am forgotten
by everybody. I wish that I might return the
compliment."

With a mere line, "She is once again in name —
as she has been ever in fact — the Ruler," Viceroy
Li, on 24th September, dismisses the *coup d'état* of
the 20th, by which Tze Hsi assumed again the full
title and responsibility for the conduct of the affairs
of the State.

At one side of the single column of written characters, which announced so briefly the startling
change in Government, is the official edict, cut from
the "Peking Gazette," the organ of the Court, of
21st September, and which in its more important
part, somewhat condensed, is as follows: —

"OUR empire is now labouring under certain great
and important stresses, and steady and wise guidance is needed in all branches of the public service.
WE ourselves have laboured diligently, night and
day, to perform OUR duties, but in spite of all OUR
anxious energy and care WE are in constant fear lest
delay should be the undoing of the country. WE
now respectfully recall the fact that Her Imperial

Majesty the Empress Dowager has on two occasions, since the beginning of the reign of H.M. T'ung-Chih, performed the functions of Regent, and that in her administrations of the Government she displayed complete and admirable qualities of perfection which enabled her successfully to cope with every difficulty that arose.

"Recollecting the serious burden of the responsibility WE owe to OUR ancestors and to the Nation, WE have repeatedly besought Her Majesty to condescend once more to administer the Government. Now she has graciously honoured US by granting OUR prayer, a blessing, a heaven-sent blessing, for all OUR subjects.

"From this day forth Her Majesty will transact the business of the Government in the Side Hall of the Palace, and on the day after to-morrow WE ourselves at the head of OUR Princes and Ministers shall perform obeisance before her in the Hall of Diligent Government.

"The Yamens concerned shall respectfully and with despatch make all such arrangements as are necessary to this ceremonial.

"The words of the Emperor.

"Given this Day."

(Without date.) — "I am in fear and trembling for what may happen in Peking and throughout the north. The old-style 'reformer' is gone, and the newer-style 'reformer' is here!

"There are whispered threats in all the departments of Government against the Christians, and I already hear rumours of disturbances in the vicinity of Paoting-fu. If the evil influences about Her Majesty are allowed to go unchecked, and political insanity reigns within the Forbidden City, I see only a few short months of national tranquillity.

"My messages of preparation have been well received by the legations, and five of them, those of England, Russia, Germany, France, and Japan, have sent notes of thanks. Minister Conger called in person, and assured me that my words, which he knows were sent to all, are reassuring."

"*Tientsin, October* 9. — A courier arriving from the capital this morning brings me many communications of great interest. Jung-lu writes of the scene in the palace when the wretched Kuang Su was made to kneel and acknowledge that he was nothing at all. Jung-lu says that Her Majesty was a veritable lioness at the ceremonies of obeisance, and treated the young Emperor worse than she has often treated unruly eunuchs.

"According to what he writes, — and he declares it to be true, — the Empress Dowager threatened Kuang Su with the loss of his life if he did not readily consent to living with the Empress Consort [Tze Hsi's niece and spy], and the Emperor said he would live with her and love her. What an outrage, when personally I know he hates the sight of her!

"And then, when Chen Fei, whom the poor
Emperor has loved . . . as any young man desires
to love his true wife, made a plea for him to Her
Majesty, the latter ordered her to be carried from
the room and cast into a lone barred chamber of one
of the administration palaces. This I regard as very
wrong. It is not enough for him to be humiliated
and degraded, even before the eyes of miserable
eunuchs and servers, but the only comfort of his
domestic life is snatched from him. Of course
Jung-lu has no sympathy with the deposed monarch,
neither has Yuan Shih-k'ai; but I am going to ask
them as the greatest favour they can do me at the
present time to prevail upon Tze Hsi to allow the
Emperor to have Chen Fei with him in his prison,
the Ocean Terrace."

There is no record that Li Hung Chang ever wrote
to the Empress Dowager or to Jung-lu or Yuan Shih-
k'ai in behalf of Chen Fei, the favourite wife of the
Emperor, she who was called, because of her beauty
of form and clearness of complexion, the "Pearl
Concubine." The unfortunate young woman was
kept under close confinement for nearly two years,
without again seeing Kuang Su, except in the presence of the Empress Dowager; and she finally met
death by being thrown down one of the wells of the
Forbidden City, by Tze Hsi's orders, as the Court
took its hurried flight upon the entrance into Peking
of the allied forces in 1900.

CHAPTER IX

RETURNING to China in 1896, after his attendance as representative of his country at the coronation of the Russian Czar, Li Hung Chang, for the first time in his memoirs, speaks of his own selection by the Throne to go to St. Petersburg, though at an earlier date in the same year he has a single line referring to a Chinese ambassador at the ceremony:

"Prince Chang Chi-chun has been chosen by the Sacred Car [Their Majesties] to represent them at the crowning of the Emperor of Russia."

Though his diary indicates that he wrote a great deal on the journey from Peking to St. Petersburg, it contains not a single comment regarding his own appointment until he is again upon Chinese soil: —

"I am back once more and my spirit is pleased, for it best fits an old man to be at home among his kind. Old men — at least I think so — are not taken up with the sights of strange things or other lands, for they are, at such an age, preparing for the sights of the Place of Seven Springs, of which they have been told so much and know so little.

."I wonder why Russia asked the Throne to send me? It was most certainly a great compliment, and I have a right to feel flattered. But Chang Chi-chun was very worthy of the honour, and he informed me

how well he was suited. Just then came word from
the Russians that my coming would please them
better. That was a blow to Chi-chun, and not very
pleasing to the Empress, but I was told that from
the very beginning I had been the choice of the
Throne.

"The Russians have for long tried to impress
me with the idea that they hold me in the highest
esteem. Perhaps they do. Anyway they may have
their motives for all this. And I have no doubt they
have; but I could tell them that my own country's
interests are above all other considerations, and if I
show favour to Russia in any matter, I do so because
I believe China will be the ultimate gainer. I have
tried in years past to make Russia realise that Korea
could not be taken from us, but the standing of that
country has been changed of late, and the Czar can
hope to gain nothing by flattering me with honours
or preferences.

"Still the coronation was a wonderful sight, even
if I must say this after having been told that I was
the centre of attraction; more so, the Czar told me,
than he himself. But all this is Western flattery,
for could I not see that the beautiful Czarina was the
eye of the peacock?

"When she spoke gracious things to me and lifted
her cup of wine toward me, and smiled, I could well
believe that that was a compliment to remember.
When I told the Empress and her ladies upon my
return about the beauties of the Russian Czar's wife,

they all said she must be even as lovely as the pictures of her which I had brought to them as tokens from the Russian Court.

"The Dowager asked me many trying questions about the Russian Court, which I tried as best I could to answer intelligently. She wanted to know if the Czarina was a political power, and if she had many eunuchs about her; but I answered that the Czarina was raising a family of her own, and even giving her breasts to her children; and that eunuchs were unknown in Russia.

"She said she wished I had learned how the Russian Empress had kept her fertility. But I told her that the Russian Empress was not at all old (only half my own age), and a very careful woman.

"I did not intend to offend Her Majesty in any way, but she told me that she would question me about Russia at some later time, and announced that she must speak with her ladies. This was Her Majesty's way of telling me the audience was at an end."

"*21st Day of the* 12th *Moon.* I have received notification that I am to forfeit one year's pay for a breach of ceremony at the palace. This is a small matter, the fine, but I should be glad to know in what respect I offended Tze Hsi."

"*21st Day of the* 12th *Moon. Later.* — Messengers from the Throne have just arrived bringing a copy of the edict conferring upon me the Order of the

Golden Dragon. The original edict was written, says the copy, by Tze Hsi herself. I am inclined to think my breach of Court etiquette was not serious to her private mind, although her official mind fined me 37,000 taels for it!

"The Order of the Golden Dragon! I am truly well pleased, although I had expected it before I went on the long journey to the Capital of Russia.

"If I was not a plain man I should quite think I was a member of the Imperial family, for the Golden Dragon is conferred (except in extraordinary cases) only upon those of the Blood. Perhaps Her Majesty conferred it upon me so I could not 'offend' in her presence again, for wearing the Golden Dragon I am privileged to kneel or not as I please. But I shall always be attentive to matters of ceremony and regard to those above me, just as I expect like evidences of respect from those who are not upon an equality with me."

A few days later the Viceroy writes: —

"Liars are the worst people in all classes, I believe. While my friends are rejoicing and sending me long letters of congratulation and many gifts, my enemies are saying that the Order of the Golden Dragon was conferred by Tze Hsi upon me only to please Russia, while the fact that I have been made to forfeit a year's pay proves conclusively that I deeply offended the Throne in the matter of etiquette. Tseng [Li's secretary] tells me that he has been approached by a number of very common people, and asked if it is true that I told the Empress that our imperial princesses would have more and better children if they followed the Czarina's example. What lies! What vicious, monkey-faced lies! Any one with sense would know that even if I dared I never would address such language to Her Majesty or the ladies of the Blood. I interest myself not at all in the inner doings of the Court, for it is enough that any man keep his own household in order.

"It is not so much that the lies have been told about me or my sayings. No; for forty years I have been forced to listen to such things; but it is that the low and ignorant, hearing such words, and knowing that the loss of a year's pay was exacted of me, will really believe I uttered such infamies. And, believing I uttered them, they will think they are true. Then there will be more scandal and talk, which is all unnecessary; for I said not one word which might, seen either through a mountain gap-way or the eye of a needle, reflect at all upon the ladies of the Court. I did praise the Russian Czarina, but I dispraised no one else."

Writing in his diary at St. Petersburg, the Grand Ambassador says among other things: —

"It has been urged upon me to return to China by way of Constantinople and the Suez Canal, but I cannot agree to this plan. Now that I have traversed all this distance, I want to go to Germany and France, then to England and the United States. There are wonders for me to lay eyes upon in all these great countries; and, besides that, there are official duties to be carried out. I am told here that I shall not be received very well in England; but it is certain they will not harm me there, nor shall I do them any injury. If the house is cold and the table not set, I need not remain, for the road is long, and the traveller who has money can turn up his nose at town constables.

"To-night I am to attend another banquet given by the Czar, which I hope will not continue as long as the one of last night. It is true they prepare foods especially for me, but they do not taste like the foods at home, or those of our own cooks which we have along. The tea, however, is the best — I brought it myself as a present to the Czar and Czarina, and Tu [his chef] tells them how to make it!"

Shortly before leaving Russia for the German capital, the Ambassador wrote: —

"On Monday we shall leave the capital of the Czar and travel toward the land of the Germans. They tell me it is many hours' ride from here to the frontier on the west, and that if we went south it would be three times as far. Going north, the Czar's dominions reach to the top of the earth, where mountains and lakes of ice are seen forever, through all the moons.

"Often and often I had studied over the maps

of the countries of the world, and I knew, of course, that Russia was a far-reaching empire; but I had to travel to know fully how immense and solid it is. There are vast plains and tremendous mountains, but there are no seas or oceans coming in between, and I cannot help thinking how much more solid and substantial this empire must be than the British Empire, with its islands and possessions scattered like fowl over a large barnyard. China is much like Russia in this respect, too, and it is sad that our nation has not yet learned how to make all parts of it stand together as one against the outsider. There is this difference between China and Russia. Many of the nations agree to harass China, but not any of them will bother Russia. If Russia did not want to control us in all our home affairs, what a strong alliance would be possible between us!

"*Sunday night.* — All the party attended a long church service this afternoon, and when it came time for my final audience with the Czar I was very fatigued. Dr. Morniff, the household physician, who has been attached to our party here by courtesy of the Government, gave me a hypodermic of something, and a large bottle of white wine, so that when we reached the castle I was feeling like a boy. I told His Majesty that the long service and the smoke of the incense nearly sickened me, at which he laughed heartily, showing his fine teeth, and said I was about the healthiest-looking man about.

"'When are Your Majesties coming to China?' I asked him.

"Again he laughed, and said that maybe sometime he would like to arrange for his wife to meet the Dowager Empress and the ladies of the latter's Court somewhere in the Far East.

"Nicholas is himself not a very healthy man, I think. I believe he stays indoors too much, or that worry about his life keeps him pale and listless. He is a small man to rule a great empire; though Napoleon, they tell me, was even smaller in stature. But there are many big men in this capital. The Czar is surrounded by them; and his soldiers, especially those regiments which are of his household, are a magnificent lot of men. I believe the Japanese soldiers would run fast from these regiments.

"I have learned that we start early to-morrow morning. This is not to my taste. I should much prefer to begin the journey now, and sleep on the train going. To arise so early in the morning seems to be a foolish Western practice; foolish especially among men of state, who could so much better transact their affairs at night when all is quiet and the mind is most alert.

"But from what I can learn, these statesmen and lawgivers look for their pleasures at night; going to banquets, theatres, and fancy parties; often staying until the light of dawn comes on again. To this I attribute much of the intrigue that is known to all these courts. The women cannot enter the council chambers nor make speeches in the parliaments, but they work their wiles at the parties and operas."

"*On the train, Monday*. — This train is travelling at a much slower pace than any of those before. I asked why, and was told that the Government would not run any risks when so many big foreign officials were aboard.

"Soldiers are everywhere along the line, and whenever the train stops the common people are kept at a distance.

"It is bad enough to be an official in China, and put up with lies, abuse, and misrepresentation; but here in Russia they kill their big officials whenever they can. I am told that a great secret band exists all over the empire, and that the members thereof find their chief occupation and 'amusement' in the killing of men of state and others in high position.

"I do not think I should like to exchange positions with the Czar, even to have the fine Czarina as wife and my choice of the rarest tea! Especially in these later years I have had no fear of my life being taken, unless it would be by some crazy fanatic like the fellow who shot me in the eye at Shimonoseki. Several times in Hankow, in the days of my first viceroyalty, low fellows sought to take my life, and once in Tientsin [when Li was Viceroy of Chihli] a low fellow came into my courtyard and told the banner captain in charge that he intended taking my life. He had a long piece of wire, and said he was going to hang me to my own gateposts. I had to have his head cut off before he would stop talking."

"*Nearing the German frontier. Hour of the Sheep.* P'lo has just finished shaving my head, and I feel fine. I think I should be insane if I wore all the hair some of these Russians do. Many of my people have chaffed me about my beard, but I wish they could see the hairy faces of the St. Petersburg Court. They are 'hairy devils' in truth!

"My mother said that as a little baby I had evidences of a strong beard later in life. She averred that it was a sign that I should be a great man in my country, and many times since affairs have gone so well with me has she asked: 'Was not my prophecy correct?' Always I have been compelled to answer her that I did not know, but if she thought I was a great man I was.

"So Napoleon marched all this distance from France in the midst of winter! He was either a very brave and determined man or a very foolish one, for even now, with the best of accommodations and soldiers to *guard* us instead of fight us, it is a long and tiresome journey. Some of the country is very beautiful, but there are hundreds of miles that are dreary wastes, and fit only for sheep and goats and even wild wolves. There are always wolves where there are sheep. It is the same in the life of man and the lives of nations.

"I do not want to be thought of as a wolf by my

fellow-men. But I have been called worse names, even to 'foreign devil,' which is ridiculous! Gordon said once that he knew it was my ambition to overthrow the Monarchy and make myself Emperor of the whole Middle Kingdom. This thought comes to me now when I am in the country Napoleon wanted to rule. Gordon was a good friend in time of need, but I was a still greater friend to him, and he could have done nothing but for my money and influence in keeping the 'Ever Victorious Army' together. I had no ambition ever to go as Emperor to the Northern Capital [Peking].

"The train is bustling with life and excitement now, for we are coming to the frontier. There are many soldiers, and the people afar off are looking at the train. We shall meet the Germans soon, as I can tell from the booming of the cannon and the music of bands.

"I wish the band music would stop, and not blare in my ears so near by. I wonder if I shall meet Herr Krupp?"

Writing in his diary a few days later, while the guest of the German Government, Li Hung Chang refers at considerable length once more to General "Chinese" Gordon, the English Commander of the "Ever Victorious Army," which Chang employed so successfully in putting down the Taiping Rebellion in 1863.

"The English will want to know just what caused

the trouble between General Gordon and myself,
and I shall have to tell them that I was not at all
jealous of him, as has been charged so many times.
Why should I be? He was directly under my orders,
and nothing pleased me better than to see him win
so many battles with the 'Ever Victorious Army,'
and drive the Wangs [leaders of the Taipings] into
Suchau. Gordon was not over-anxious for the end
of the rebellion, and I knew that he had secretly
memorialised the Throne to make him general-in-
chief of all the armies of China, including those of the
different viceroys. He did not know that no person
had power to grant him such unlimited authority,
and his foreign pride made him think he was above
myself in power. He made mistakes, and many
of them; but I overlooked them all, thinking only
of the great good he had rendered the country.

"His final mistake, however, I could not overlook,
and my memorial to the Throne was the cause of
his dismissal forever from the service of China.

"This grievous mistake of his was the accusation
that I had treacherously caused the murder of the
Wangs upon my own barge. The very truth of this
matter is here written for the second time; the first
time was in my report to the Grand Council at the
Northern Capital, made in the year 1866, just before
I myself took the field against the Shantung rebels.

"Mow Wang told the other Wangs at Suchau that
he would not surrender to the Imperial forces but
would continue fighting for ten years. He was killed

upon this statement, and Chung Wang sent word to me that he intended to surrender. I immediately informed my own lieutenant, General Ching; and Chung Wang and eight other generals, with their men, surrendered. We were most friendly disposed when the fighting was all over, and it was myself who proposed that we have a feast in celebration. To this Chung Wang, Lar Wang, and General Ching quickly assented; and soon the banquet was set on board my private boat.

"In the meantime, General Gordon, who thought he had not been accorded full glory for the complete surrender of the Taipings, moved the 'Ever Victorious Army' away from Suchau to its old headquarters at Quinsan. This was against my orders, and also against the counsel of General Chang; but Gordon claimed there was a large amount of pay due him and his men. This was true, but it was also true that he had not been promised, and should not have expected, pay until the Suchau army had surrendered. He was feeling ill-disposed, and was waiting for replies to his memorials sent to the Throne. His last memorial, as I knew through See Lund H'en, who wrote it, was very much against me.

"When the banquet was set and we were in the midst of our joyousness, report was brought me that two large boats had pulled out from the shore and were coming directly to my boat. I went to the near side and looked. It was about the hour of the cock [7 P.M.], and I could not discern plainly, but it seemed to me as if Gordon himself captained one of the boats. I went back to the feast and told the Wangs I believed Gordon was coming. Ching turned very white and whispered to me that he was afraid — of what, he did not say; but before we, Ching, Lar Wang, and myself, had time to reach that end of the boat which was pointed to the shore, Imperial officers and soldiers clambered aboard from both sides and began cutting every one they met. They killed Lar Wang by my side, and one fellow stabbed General Ching, but only slightly. An officer was coming toward me with his sword, but he fell to his knees when I raised my hand.

"Ching, Lu'Klen, Tu-Kiang, General Tung, and myself all succeeded in getting into one of the soldier boats and the pole-man pushed us to the shore. Immediately I issued orders to all the troops in the city to make an attempt to capture those of the attacking party; but the feeling against the Wangs was so strong that I think but little attempt was made to carry out my orders. That night I learned that all the members of the banqueting party remaining aboard were decapitated and their bodies thrown into the river. Among these were a deep personal friend whom I loved very much, and a young nephew of mine from Wu-Sang.

"I will have Fong Lee [his English secretary] make a translation of this, and a number of copies; and if I am asked anything about this in England this true statement will be the answer."

Evidently the Viceroy was not questioned regarding the Wang massacre by his English entertainers, for this line appears among his notes made two weeks later on board the Atlantic liner: —

"Only Gladstone mentioned Gordon to me in England. I guess most people have forgotten him."

CHAPTER X

DURING the first five days of his stay in Germany the Viceroy did not write a line in his diary, though he does not fail to cover his experiences there pretty thoroughly when he again "takes pen in hand"; or rather, quill, for he was most proficient in the use of the latter, seldom, if ever, in his official or more important writings, using the stick or camel's-hair brush so commonly employed by his countrymen.

He writes at Essen: "While I am officially the guest of the German nation, I am personally the guest of Herr Krupp, whom I have for many years longed to see. I do not know which I had the greater desire to see, Prince Bismarck or Herr Krupp; but however that may be, I have seen them both, talked with them freely, and feel that, had no other attraction or benefit been awaiting me in Germany, I have been well repaid. Each of these men seems to be filling the place he is best fitted to occupy: Krupp, in his quiet way, making big guns, and Bismarck occupying a place where he can put them into use. For, while it is known that the Kaiser is the head and front of Germany, yet it is Bismarck who is the solid rock upon which any great trouble must fall.

"I had a splendid visit with Prince Bismarck at

his castle, day before yesterday. He made me drink some beer, which I did not like at all, but a taste for which he said I should acquire if I stayed long enough in Germany. I told him I did not expect to live many years longer, and that it would probably be impossible for me to acquire a liking for the national beverage.

"We smoked our pipes together and enjoyed a long visit, troubled only by those who translated for us and by the servants who brought pipes and drinkables. During a large part of the time we discussed international policies, and finally came to the prospective influence of Germany in the Far East.

"'You have seen but little of us in your part of the world,' he said, 'for Germany as a unit is only a new nation; but the time will come when the German Empire will dominate Europe. England, with all her bluster and show, has a hundred weak points; and she knows that a conflict with a power nearly her equal will mean her undoing. I hate the boasting Englanders even though German blood rules from the throne.'

"When, toward the end of our meeting, in fact as we were about to part, I told him that some people had paid me the high compliment of calling me the 'Bismarck of the Far East,' the Prince tried to look serious as if studying my meaning. Then he smiled under his bushy eyebrows and whispered to Captain Ruffbach (who spoke the best Mandarin Chinese I ever heard a German use). 'Tell His Excellency that the French would not consider that a compliment at all!' Of course I understood, and we shook hands over the agreement that the French did not love Bismarck.

"I found that the Prince could deliver a compliment as quickly as any one, for he immediately said after our handshake, 'And so they have called Your Excellency the Bismarck of the East, eh? Well, I want to tell you that I cannot ever hope to be termed the "Li Hung Chang of Europe!"'

"As I was coming to Essen from Berlin, we naturally spoke a good deal regarding Herr Krupp, who Bismarck said was an emperor in his own way, the 'Emperor of Essen.' 'Germany is not for war,' he said, 'but strong armament is as necessary to a nation as a club is to a policeman. The policeman does not carry his stick to use upon the heads of innocent people, but he has it in plain sight so that evilly inclined persons may know that he is always prepared for trouble. Let the policeman walk his beat carrying a feather or a wisp of hay and see how quickly the bullies will jump upon him and rob him of the little he possesses.

"'And so with Essen. Herr Krupp has established a great industrial plant there and provided bread and beer for thousands. Even if not one of his guns was ever fired he would still be a great benefactor of his country. But as it is, he is still greater from the German point of view. He has won many victories for his country, victories that the public know nothing about. The noise of Essen to-day is the song of peace; to-morrow it may be the voice of a united Germany speaking through a thousand Essen mouths to an enemy.'

"Captain Ruffbach accompanied me here by the request of Bismarck, and I am glad he did, for he seems to know about everything, and is able to tell what he knows. The captain was for many years employed at Peking and Canton in consular capacities, and writes well in Chinese. I think I shall ask the Kaiser to send him back with me.

"Herr Krupp presented me with a fine steel-framed painting of himself yesterday. I asked for it because of my great admiration for him. He said that Müller had painted the picture for his wife (Madame Krupp), but that she was delighted to let me have it. Herr Krupp also made me a present of a complete miniature battery of artillery, of a good size for children to play with. In fact, he had them drawn into my room by six little school-girls all dressed in yellow and hauling the little cannons by yellow silk ribbons. One of the little girls thought it was real war, I imagine, for she was very much frightened and after a while began to cry. And she was the one that 'drove' the others, too; and probably was captain of the battery. I could not help thinking that that was often the way, for I remember that once while fighting the Tongs in Senchi we had officers that were mere cowards, while the common men would fight bravely.

"Herr and Madame Krupp, General Vonzberg, Count and Countess Gregg and others were present when the gift of the battery of artillery was made and accepted. I spoke in reply to Herr Krupp's brief speech and Captain Ruffbach translated it excellently. But he overlooked my last sentence, and I called his attention to it. He grew very red in the face and it was evident that he was somewhat embarrassed, but I only repeated my statement, and he in turn gave it to the little company. Poor fellow, he thought it was going to offend the party!

"But as soon as Ruffbach's words were out of his mouth, the whole company burst into laughter, and Herr Krupp actually slapped me upon the shoulder and acted like a merry brother.

"'You shall have one; yes, a real battery!' he said a couple of times. You see I had told him that while I appreciated highly his compliment to myself as the representative of the Chinese Throne and people, I believed his great gun-works would be made better known in Eastern Asia by a battery of big guns!

"And so this morning at the works six finely polished guns were paraded before me as the present of Herr Krupp to the Chinese Empire, a gift worth more than 108,000 taels! But I do not think he will lose by his generosity, for Lord C'lung has instructed two of the German engineers here to select three other batteries of field-pieces and four ten-inch guns to be shipped at an early date to China. We shall buy German powder and shells here also."

"*Next day. Hour of the Drake.* — This day I shall seclude myself from all callers, in order that I may devote myself to thoughts of my celestial mother, who died fourteen years ago this day, and who for that long time has been thinking of my coming to the Peaceful Sunlight of the Nine Springs. With all the incidents of my life, its trials and lamentations, its moments of joy and pride, with each and every affair of life, I cannot forget my celestial mother and all she was and is to me.

"My father died many years before my mother, and his grave is great and hallowed. Many hundreds of times did my mother bless it and ask my father's spirit to hurry the time when her own might join his in the Happy Vale of Ancestral Longevity. My mother could never think of taking her own life. It is thought great and glorious to do such a thing by many of the ignorant, — and many of the intellectual, too, — but my father's beloved helpmeet could never think it was right, nor that it pleased the spirits of the gone-before.

"In my early days I was possessed of many ideas that I know now were foolish and wicked, and not at all in agreement with common sense or philosophy; one of these is suicide, and another is the putting out of the way of infants. If a man or woman has lost his or her face [i.e., is disgraced] so badly that it is impossible to retrieve it, then perhaps it is better to be buried deep in the earth than to live and see shame all the rest of one's days. Or, if a government official, with many honours bestowed upon him, is caught stealing the money that belongs to the Throne, and cannot pay back all that he has taken, even to the last cash, it is better that he take poison. For by doing so he will be thought better of by his family and friends and by the Government. But if he will persist in living, even when the law of his punishments do not reach him, he is each day a greater disgrace than he was the day before; and upon his family the burden is heavier as each hour passes.

"Or, if a great official, when he finds that his country is humiliated through him, even though personally he be not at fault, it is a true sign of great love of country if he put an end to his life. For what happiness can a man have when he knows that that name which he so proudly bore is the name to be forever linked with some defeat or degradation of his country's?

"I can bless the name of my great and noble friend Admiral Ting, and I can bow before the grave of the illustrious General Chang! And I can burn incense to the spirit of the gallant Commodore Liu! [Officers who committed suicide after the capture of Wei-hai-wei by the Japanese, in January, 1895.] Yes, they are honoured by all the world even in defeat, and their spirits are sweetest and happiest among those of our noble ancestors! Yes, even the Japanese, in their hour of material victory over our brave men on land and sea, did not refrain from doing great honour to these glory-laden officers of our army and navy. [The writer here refers to the honour paid the suicide officers by Admiral Ito, the Japanese commander, who restored one of the captured Chinese vessels to be a ship of honour for the conveying home of their bodies.]

"I did not ever care much for the Japanese, and a deadly hatred was in my heart against that nation when it forced China into war over Korea, which for two thousand years had been ours; but I loved Marquis Ito for this noble action, and I was ready to treat with him in the arrangement of peace.

"Such causes for self-destruction are sufficient, but many people take their lives for less reason than would be necessary to send a vagrant to jail for two days. They are silly people; they act only from silly and selfish motives; they have much pride and self-love, and they want others to think they are brave. Many widows cut their throats or bind twine tightly about their necks or their bowels, or swallow large doses of poisonous herbs, in an attempt to show what affection they have for their departed husbands. What a silly thing! especially if that were the reason; but the truth is that the widow has become lazy, or she fears no other man will want to work for her support. In this she does not deceive herself, neither does she fool the many thousands who are glad to come and witness her death. Let the widow marry again and rear up more spirits to honour the spirits of those gone before. Of course, if she is too lazy to do this, suicide is good enough for her.

"When I was a very young boy in Anhuei I was accused of something wrong, and some of my youthful friends told me that I could only save my face and the face of my family by jumping into a well. I was guilty of the wrong — the taking of two ducks from a pond, which I cooked and ate — and I was very sorry, even without the severe punishment administered to me by my father and mother as well as by the owner of the fowl. But I did not want to die, although I had disgraced my people and myself. I went to my mother to ask her if I should jump into the well. She said, No; that it would not be right; but that the better thing for me to do would be to earn enough in the next harvest time to pay for the ducks and to give an extra duck and seven eggs besides. This advice I followed, paying my debts and more — for I gave a fine rabbit to the magistrate, and ever after that he was my friend.

"My life's greatest grief was the death of my mother, and I desired a year of mourning; but the Throne had negotiated with Russia as to the status of Korea, and I was compelled to be in constant communication with the Tsung Li Yamen.

"A letter from Von Moltke has just been handed me by Song. I shall read it to-morrow. To-night I must read long into the hours from the philosophers in memory of my mother.

"The little battery of artillery, all its mouths

pointing east-north [northeast], seems to say that if
we ever fight the Japanese again we shall be better
prepared. The toy guns please that part of my nature which is of the boy. But the business battery
present is a joy indeed!

"I now (8 P.M.) take up the Mang-tsze for a five
hours' reading."

"*Morning.* — The letter from Von Moltke is
simply one expressing his desire to meet me when I
arrive at Potsdam. He was to have been at Scheven-
ingen. (I can scarcely write that horrible name.)

"But I shall never forget the wonderful display of
sky-fire [fireworks] the people of that place prepared
for me. We have many kinds of coloured sky-fires
in China, and they are truly wonderful, but what I
saw at S. [a mark in the diary] was as if all the spirits
of the air had combined to make a home show for
me in Europe. There were real battles of men and
ships. I know, because I have seen them. And there
were great representations of the Golden Dragon, a
picture of the Empress Grand Dowager [Tze Hsi] and
of the Emperor. At last they had, with the booming
of cannons and the blare of many military bands,
a picture of His Excellency Li Hung Chang, in his
yellow jacket! And, without knowing, of course,
what kind of a show I was to witness — although
I had been informed in advance that it was in my
honour — I had donned my yellow jacket early that
evening, and was attired in it when the Army Com-

mittee, headed by General Von Getner (?) and the city committee, headed by Burgomeister Sanders called — "

In a marginal note, written some time later, the Viceroy explains that he was interrupted in his description of the "feast of S." by the arrival of one of his party with a number of important cablegrams, one of them being from President Cleveland inviting him to America in the name of the American people. This message also enquired on behalf of the State Department the probable time of the Viceroy's arrival in the United States.

"*Bremerhaven* (*three or four days after leaving Potsdam*). — From all that I have seen, I am more than ever convinced that the Kaiser and Prince Bismarck meant what they said when they averred that the German Empire was destined to become a dominant factor in Europe. I am wonderfully impressed with the way this nation seems to be working as a unit. The army is upon a business basis, the navy is on a business basis, and the whole machinery of government works smoother than our best Canton timepieces.

"I arrived here this morning, accompanied by a host of high officials, and others met our party here. The whole place is in gala attire, and I have all I can do to make myself believe that I am only a foreigner visiting the country, instead of a king in this land.

I am told that hundreds and thousands of foreigners are here to-day, and a great number have been introduced to me, some English, some French, and some Americans — the latter said to be so rich that they could buy the fleet of magnificent warships lying in this fine harbour.

"It is a long time since I was engaged in any fighting, hand to hand, and I am now getting too aged to think of engaging in it; nevertheless, my eyes never tire of regiments of soldiers and great warships that can do things.

"In answer to my questions I have learned the approximate cost of most of the German ships. There are great shipyards here, and Germany intends to build all her navy for all time at home. I could wish for nothing better than that China should build her own fleet and have every man and officer in it a true son of the Middle Kingdom; but our people are not sailors, except upon the rivers, and they do not know how to handle machinery. But they will learn in time, I hope. Anyway, when I return, I shall make it my duty to urge advancement in all Western arts and crafts. We have our beautiful literature, far and away ahead of that of the Western nations; but they have the money and the guns.

"It was a sad thought for me to-day, as I saw those fine ships lying idle there, that they were doing no particular good, while, if they had been ours, we should have conquered the Japanese!

"Some of the officials hinted that I ought to leave an order at Bremerhaven for one or two ships, and I said to one of the admirals standing by: 'If you will sell me that ship over there for 2,300,000 taels I will go in her to France and England and America.' But he said that my naval knowledge was too good; I had picked out his flagship, the strongest battle-ship of the German navy."

"*Two days later.* — We are in France, and somehow I am feeling more at home. My stomach is in bad shape, for I have been tempted to eat too much of German foods. Maybe it is the wines that trouble me, for I have been taking much of their white wines, and like them so well that Count Hatzfeldt said he would ship many casks to Tientsin for me.

"Seventy-five thousand Frenchmen surrendered to the Germans just where we crossed into France."

CHAPTER XI

"LA BELLE FRANCE, they call this country," Viceroy Li wrote on the evening of the second day in Paris; "the beautiful France, I am told it means, and I am ready to agree with the sentiment. Indeed, from my observations, I will go still further, and call it Happy and Beautiful and Gracious France, for in all my travels no hours have been so pleasing to me as those which I have spent in this delightful land.

"Perhaps there is a sense of patriotism in this thought, for I must confess that much of the country between Metz and Paris is considerably like that of Kuang-Tung and Kuang-Su provinces. Of course, there is a vast difference in the houses and fences, and the people are not at all alike; but the panorama from the train for miles and miles was of the more lovely portions of central and south China. The trees and vegetables and grasses seem to have the same greens and other colours, and if the houses were changed and hidden from view, and if a few of my people stood along the railroad, I could easily think I was one or two hundred miles from Canton instead of being that distance from Paris.

"And this is the very country through which the mighty German armies, headed by the King of Prussia and the master strategist, my friend Von

Moltke, and directed by that man of silent thunder and terrible lightning, Prince Bismarck, — who offered me so much *hofbrau* only the other day, — marched to the subjugation and humiliation of the proud country of Napoleon. It is most interesting to think about these things, but I suppose the French people would rather forget.

"In truth I believe they must have long since forgotten, for these people are what we call in Chinese a smiling family. They are so different from the Russians and the Germans — I mean the masses. Russian crowds seem to have no enthusiasm. There is respect and awe of a dull kind in their faces, and a sort of hopelessness that they seem to be afraid to give expression to. With the Germans there is enthusiasm, but it is of a hard, matter-of-fact kind — the life of business or science, perhaps. They laugh a great deal, sing much, and talk loud; but somehow I was given the impression that all these three came from their beers and wines, more than from the heart or soul.

"But the French, as I have said, are so different. The faces of the crowds, even of the little boys and girls, seem to be those of a people who are living a life of earnest joy, as if they knew there was much good pleasure in life, and intended to get it out without making too hard a job of it.

"This morning I paid a brief visit to the Bank of France, and met the board of governors, all of them introduced by M. Leroux, of the Ministry of Finance.

I was interested in this great institution, which they tell me owns financially one half the kings and princes of Europe. I wonder if I could borrow a few million francs? As a bit of humour, I had C'Lung ask that question when we were in the executive rooms, and the chief governor immediately replied: 'Yes, Your Excellency, fifty millions, almost on your own terms!' Then I told him that I was not serious about it, and to this he replied that when China was serious about loans the Bank of France would be ready.

"For more than an hour I enquired into the system of finance in vogue in France, and it is, I believe, the simplest yet most perfect in the world. I was astounded when M. Leroux told me that if every centime were taken from the vaults for governmental purposes, a call on the branch banks throughout France for 1,000,000,000 taels would be answered satisfactorily within forty-eight hours. I wonder if this can be true?

"I learn that loan-offices [pawn-shops] are almost unknown in France. My enquiries regarding them appeared to amuse my informants, for it has been published widely in the Parisian papers (and I presume in the English and American press, too) that my own wealth is largely invested in the pawn-shop business of China; and one of the illustrated French papers, thinking it was humorous, pictured me yesterday with a Jewish nose and holding in one hand the Western symbol of the loan office. Monsieur Chateauvère, the chief of the French secret police detailed to guard me while in Paris, asked if I wanted legal proceedings against the publisher to be taken, but I told him that I had enjoyed the cartoon as much, probably, as any one.

"It seems that in the Western world the small moneylender, or perhaps, better, the lender of small sums, is a person despised by the general public. That is because they squeeze the blood of those who borrow. That is why the 'pawn-broker' is an undesirable person in the community.

"However, I can say that while many of the statements made regarding me as the owner of most of the loan offices in China are without doubt much exaggerated, I am interested largely in such establishments in some of the provinces. Nor am I ashamed of such interest. On the contrary, I am glad that I have so often been able to help poor people with small loans, upon either their goods, their labour, or just their promises. It is not seemly that I write of my own virtues, but it is surely the privilege and duty of every man to defend his name and character when attacked. Therefore, I will say that though I have made a comfortable amount of wealth from my loan-offices, it has not been made by excessive interest charges. If I had been a hard man to all those who had borrowed from my agents and were unable to pay, I should to-day be one of the richest men in the world. And then, too, I have never used what wealth was graciously given me by the good gods for evil purposes. I have bought neither honours nor offices. I would cut my face with a knife rather than accept an office or an honour by purchase.

"It is true that I have loaned large sums to the provinces, and even to the Throne, but it is also true that certain honours were stripped from me when the Government was greatest in my debt. It is also true that for many years I have contributed well to flood or drought sufferers, and it is on record at the Room of Worthy Deeds [Peking] that during the last direful famine I supplied food to one thousand families in Tientsin, to four thousand families in other parts of Chihli, and to five hundred families in Shantung, for more than sixteen weeks. . . .

"They tell me there is very little poverty in France, and that even the poorest people save a little from day to day."

"*Tuesday evening.* — This evening I was received by the President of the Republic and Madame Faure. The great halls of the President's palace were thronged with eminent people from all over France and Europe. The American Minister was there, and extended personally an invitation on the part of President Cleveland. I know, from all I have heard, seen, and learned, that my reception in America will be most agreeable. I look forward to it anxiously, especially to seeing New York and Washington, and visiting with Mr. Cleveland.

"The French President is a quiet man, of studious, careful habits, I should think. He had learned somewhere or somehow to speak one or two phrases in Chinese and these he repeated at least eight times during our first meeting. Madame Faure is a plain woman, but, I hear, of very kindly heart. She had around her at the reception a number of the most beautiful ladies I had ever seen. They were duchesses, princesses, countesses, and the daughters of plain politicians or merchants; but they were all so charming that the title of Empress would not be too great for the majority.

"What strange things do happen! One of the gentlemen standing at a distance seemed familiar to me, and I found after a while that he was almost staring at me, as if to attract my particular attention to him. When I asked Tuan to find out who he was, the gentleman himself came over and extended his hand in European fashion. 'Does Your Excellency remember me?' he asked in my own language. The moment he spoke I remembered him. He was Captain Fournier, now a high official, who was the representative of France at the Tientsin Treaty. I was so glad to see him again, for he is truly a chivalrous man and an honour to his country! I will send him a chest of tea.

"*Midnight, before starting for Calais.* — Tuan opened and read to me a long letter from the German Kaiser a little while ago. It came through the German Embassy here, and informs me that my request for

sent to their staterooms by the nasty little Narrow Sea of the English."

During the first four days in England, so completely taken up was Li Hung Chang's time, as he himself tells, so busy was he "with small things and great, small people and famous," that he had no time for his memoirs.

"*Hawarden, Eleventh Day in Memory of the Peaceful Jade Emperor.* — Only here, in the home of the greatest living Englishman, have I found real rest since leaving the boat at Dover. Here I have enjoyed for a day such a rest as I have not known since bidding good-bye to China; for it is a pleasurable rest to see and know this 'Grand Old Man.' It is delightful to learn his thoughts and to see things of this world as he sees them. It is the highest prize of public service to be able to retire to such a home life as is his, amid the respect of the world and the love and admiration of his countrymen. If I could be any other person than Li Hung Chang I should want to be William Ewart Gladstone, the Grand Old Man of England. And I should like best of all women, even now before the Czarina, one of Fournier's lovely daughters.

"Mr. Gladstone met me at the handsome, green-covered station upon my arrival. A great crowd of his countrypeople were there, and hats were raised and handkerchiefs fluttered while our party descended from the train. Then there was long and hearty applause as we shook hands, both of us bareheaded. I do not know when before, in public, I have been seen without a head covering.

"Mr. Gladstone — he is only 'mister,' for he has refused the highest titles the British Queen could bestow — was much stronger in appearance than I had expected to find him; yet, when we were close together and sat face to face, I could see that he was an old man; much older in his face than I, although there is but nine years' difference, I believe, in our ages.

"At once he apologised for not having come to London to meet me. But he said that if he had made the trip he would very likely have been ill for a week or two. He had sent a telegram to me at Windsor Castle to this same effect, two days before, and so I had determined to visit him at Hawarden; even at the expense of offending a number of the entertainment committee and several members of the House of Lords who had given me pressing invitations to visit their homes."

The Viceroy on a later date gives a list of the different personages in England who he thought might be offended because he had chosen to go "of his own will" to visit Gladstone at Hawarden, while neglecting to accept the many other urgent invitations to prominent houses.

"What had these other people to offer me?" he

asks. "Bread and wine and musical entertainments? I had never heard of them, any of them, and what should I be spending my time with them for? The Queen, Her Majesty Victoria, of England and Ireland and India, her son, who will be King if he lives, Mr. Gladstone, Mr. Morley, Lord Tennyson, and the Houses of Parliament, those were what interested me in England, and the ships."

Still continuing his narrative at Hawarden, he says:—

"Mr. Gladstone and myself, accompanied only by Long-li and Bruce [interpreters and secretaries], took a long stroll over his estate, and talked of many matters removed from state affairs. I was surprised how well he knew my life, and he expressed the same feeling when I told him that which I knew regarding himself. He spoke about the Queen, about Indian affairs and of Home Rule for Ireland; and I was certain that he hoped to see that unhappy country governed better before he died. 'They have given their best to England,' he said, 'and in return have been given only England's worst.'

"He pointed out some tree-stumps to me, and said that in eight years he had kept his health good and muscles strong by this chopping exercise. It amused me very much, and I told him I would like to see him strike a blow. So he took up the instrument for cutting and made several great dents in one of the trees. Then he turned to me and said:

'Lord Li, did you ever cut down a tree?' I told him I had many a time when I was a boy, but that like many other boyish habits I had outgrown this one also. But he wanted me to try and I did. However, it was awkward work, for the handle of the instrument caught in my sleeve and I nearly cut my foot."

"*On the train, Hour of the Crow.* — I slept two hours during my visit to Mr. Gladstone, and he slept also during that time.

"When we met again a nice little lunch was served. Rare oolong, some Chinese crackers, and cold fowl. Mr. Gladstone and myself ate alone this time. Then, just before leaving, we sat together and were photographed. I could not get one of the pictures, although I would willingly pay any price for it. Still, I am told it will be in all the London papers in the morning."

During the following two days the memoirs contain only the briefest comments on the dinner given in his honour by the Lord Mayor of London, his visit to the Tower and the Houses of Parliament, and finally a carriage ride through the poorer sections of the city. Referring to this last, he says among other things: —

"Of course, it is but natural that the hosts of our party want to show us only the beautiful and prosperous in their realm. I saw great grandeur and much wealth at Moscow and St. Petersburg, the temples, parks, and fine avenues. I saw also the strength and greatness of Berlin, and the wonderful activity of Essen, Bremerhaven, Munich, and other cities. Nevertheless, my eyes were constantly watching for insights into the real conditions of the people, and I saw things that somehow told me that all was not sunshine and glory.

"And it is so with London and England. I dined as the guest of Her Majesty at the castle, and great officers of state took me to the Parliament and to the forts and arsenals. I saw the fine parks of London and some of the great thoroughfares; yet I could see in the vast crowds so many people who were poor. Even in the short time of my journey I have learned to distinguish between the different classes of people by the clothes they wear.

"My entertainers were not over-pleased, I fear, by my desire and request to be taken for even a brief period through the poorer sections. 'We have poor in China, millions of them, and the sight of rags is not new to me; but I have seen so many grand sights that I am afraid, unless you grant my wish, that to leave in my present frame of mind would mean that I had not a true conception of life in England.' It was this way that I talked to them. And finally I was shown, hurriedly, some of the poorer parts of the city.

"I cannot tell now of all I saw, nor of my fullest impressions; but I know that I have come to the conclusion that under a grand show many of the countries with great armies and fleets of ships have much misery hidden from the eyes of the world. China is not the only country where there are rags and hunger. The Chinaman cries out when his stomach is empty and his throat dry; but in foreign lands the hungry man steals from his neighbour or breaks into his house. Often, very often, as I have learned in these few but eye-and-mind-opening weeks, he is ready to make silent war with bomb or knife upon the Government he blames for his hopeless condition. The more I see and learn of the lower classes of people in Europe, the greater is my love and pity for the miserable poor of my own country; for, by comparison, the latter are less vicious. I bow now in respect to all of China — from Her Illustrious Majesty and the Court to the rivermen of Canton."

"*On the ship ready to sail for New York.* — Goodbye to you, Czar and Czarina, and to you, Russia; good-bye to you, Kaiser, Bismarck, and my friend Herr Krupp of Essen; good-bye to Happy and Gracious La Belle France; good-bye to Victoria, the Queen, and the Grand Old Man.

"I am going to Grant's country."

CHAPTER XII

THAT the Grand Ambassador to the Czar's coronation was troubled again with what he had already characterised, crossing the English Channel, as a "disordered stomach," due to the "eating of German foods," and, perhaps, to "Bismarck's hofbrau," is evident from the first entry in his diary after taking the Cunarder at Liverpool: —

"*Third day on a mad ocean.* — After eating. I do not think, if ever I went to Germany again, I would eat either with the Kaiser, Prince Bismarck, or any other great man; that is, unless he would be agreeable to my taking my own foods in my own way. For I find that my stomach has not been so disordered for years. I do not remember that I was ever so sick before. Dr. Gray, the ship's medical officer, says that I have been seasick. It is a ridiculous and most unscientific diagnosis of my case, and I did not hesitate to tell him so. Dr. Tong-le does not agree with Dr. Gray, and his disagreement gives me more faith than ever in our Chinese medics.

"The master of the vessel has been very attentive to me; more so, indeed, than I really desired — for when one feels as I have felt in the last three days, he wishes most of all to be left alone.

"Tong-le says he has never known me to be so

irritable, and my good cook says he has been unable
to please me. Poor fellow! he has staggered about the
ship like a man filled with strong drink, and I know
he is not any happier than I am. But *he* is seasick;
for he can demolish all kinds of foods, foreign and
Chinese, without experiencing the least ill-effects
afterwards.

"The sun is bright and warm to-day, and I am
beginning to enjoy the ocean air. We shall be half
the distance to America by to-night, they tell me.
I am also told that this mad ocean is quieter on the
American side."

"*Fifth day out.* — If the people aboard this ship
are a fair sample of the great mass of Americans
I am sure they are a wonderful nation. The men
are as polite as the French, and do not stare at one
like the Londoners. I was not pleased with the
crowds of England's capital. They were rough in
looks and in behaviour, and many low fellows did
actually try to insult me. But the police were everywhere vigilant and superbly organised, and several
times the thugs were taught good lessons with clubs.

"I think every one on board this ship, excepting
the third-class passengers and some of the crew,
have been presented to me in one way or another.
Fine old men, said to be the very rich, are among
the passengers. One of them, who owns many
railroads, was introduced by an American army
colonel, and later he brought his wife and daughter.

The latter is the belle of the ship, and would do for a princess at court. I told the interpreter to tell her so, and she replied with all the sweetness in the world that she would like to be if I were king!

"I think that was the highest praise I ever heard, and I shall send Miss Marvin enough fine silks for the rest of her life. She gave me a beautiful fan, which she said she had purchased in Italy. It was so rich and expensive that I did not want to take it, and so told her. But she insisted, and I kissed her hand. I have never before kissed a strange lady's hand, — not outside of our Northern Capital,— but I saw much of it in St. Petersburg and Moscow. I think now that the Czarina expected me to kiss her hand when she extended it immediately after the ceremony of the coronation, but I neglected to do it through my ignorance and excitement. Instead I placed in her hand the Precious Queen Jade Ring which the Dowager had sent as a present.

"I shall never forget the first apparent embarrassment of the Czar and his Consort, to be immediately followed by a most pleased look upon the lovely face of the pale Czarina. In a glance she examined the Precious Ring, and then gladly extended her hand once more, the ring upon her finger. I was excited somewhat, and took the hand in both of mine and knelt upon the rug. I suppose there is no man with his eyes open who will not learn something every day. Even Confucius said that a thousand years of study was only a preparation for the real knowledge one should possess to be able to stand among his ancestors."

"*A Christian holiday [Sunday]*. — My teeth are troubling me to-day; that is, those which are not false. When I get to Shanghai again I shall have these last troubling ones removed. We shall be in New York to-morrow. I feel thirty years younger than Gladstone."

"*At evening, Second Hour of the Crow.* — I shall go to my bed early, for we shall be in New York Harbour at daylight. I am worried about this American life I must lead for two or three weeks. I hope it will be much shorter. I only want to see Cleveland, and the tomb of General Grant."

It is exactly a week, according to the diary, before His Excellency takes up again the narrative of his trip, writing at the Hotel Bellevue, Philadelphia: —

"How can I write of all that has happened in the six days just past? It seems as if I had lived a year or more since I landed in New York from the Atlantic steamer. I have been tired almost beyond words, but the reception I have been accorded by this great American people has filled me with pride, and I know that in China it will be thought most wonderful.

"And is it not strange? For years my people have

been barred out of this rich country — not because they were criminals or had leprosy, but just because they were born in China. If the same persons had been born in Japan or Korea or India or England they would have been let pass through the emigrant gates. And yet, I was born in China, and these Americans, high and low, pay me the honour and attention due a visiting monarch. I will see if this cannot be changed somewhat.

"I have met that great-and-everywhere person known as the American newspaper man, and I have enjoyed him. Also, I guess, he has enjoyed me, for I have been told more funny things by the reporters than I ever heard in all my life before. They are a jolly lot of fellows, and I think a regiment of them would make the biggest army [enemy] laugh so much that they either could not fight, or would not want to shoot such clever chaps.

"When we came sailing into New York Bay, — before, indeed, we had really left the mad ocean behind us, — there were many craft coming to meet us, smoke from their funnels, and white steam and noise from their whistles. Ahead of all the rest were two or three handsome launches, making for our ship as if they would run us down. I thought these must be the official boats, and I went far forward on the ship and looked ahead to the oncoming vessels.

"There were no ladies on these first boats, and I surely thought they must be the carriers of the officials. But I soon learned my mistake, for these were the boats of the American press. Our big ship slowed down — for the press is all-powerful in the United States — and a lot of men scrambled aboard. They were clean, fine-looking fellows; like young diplomats or secretaries in a foreign office.

"At first I was somewhat nonplussed at their familiarity, for they neither bowed nor hung back, but came straight to our party, and began introducing themselves and shaking hands. It was impossible to be offended, although, as I have said, I was at a loss just what to do or say. But soon I got used to the fine fellows, and took them as far forward on the deck as we could go.

"When I had them there I said: 'Now, gentlemen, I have come to see America, and not to be the distributor of information. I want to learn things. Therefore, please tell my secretaries all about the points of interest as we go up the harbour.' And they did it, too. I asked about everything I saw, and before we had landed in New York I could tell many things concerning the city, especially what buildings loomed up into the sky, the various waters of the bay, the islands, and the forts, and a lot of such information as only one who travels may acquire.

"From that morning to this I have not been — I was going to say an instant — an hour, in my waking life, without the company of my newspaper friends. At Washington, with the officials, on the

trains, at all the receptions and meetings, even waiting for me at the hotels when I wanted to retire, and
again looking for me before I had partaken of the
first morning meal — they are wonderful and tireless, and deserve to earn a great deal of money. I
saw them hobnobbing with the President and with
Governors, just as if these high officials were only
respectable tax-gatherers. Still, it all told me that
this country was, indeed, the democracy of the
world. That great lesson I learned from the actions
of the American newspaper men, and I bless them
for it!

"I am a journalist myself. Many people would be
willing to doubt and to ridicule, but it is true nevertheless. While I have never published a journal, nor
acted as editor, the profession of writing is so noble
that I am honoured to claim membership therein.
When in my youth I thought of my future, I said
that some day I wanted to be the Chang-yuan [poet-
laureate] of my country, and I studied long and diligently. I took my degrees ahead of many thousands,
the hsui-tsai [A.B.], the chu-jen [M.A.], and the
tsun-sz [LL.D.], following each other rapidly. And
I have written and written for many years.

"One young reporter laughed long when I told
him I was a newspaper man, too, and that he surely
did not expect me to give him all the information I
had gathered. He had been asking me questions like
a rapid-fire gun, and I saw he was new at his profession, and I pitied him.

"'You say, Mr. Li Hung Chung, that you are a newspaper man?' he asked when I appeared serious.

"'Yes,' I replied, 'I have written a great deal that has been published in our Chinese papers, and which the editors did not dare refuse.'

"'How was that?' he enquired.

"'They were decrees from the Throne,' I told him.

"Evidently that was all he needed for his article that day; for he left me immediately, after offering me a cigar, and the next morning I read in one of the New York papers that '*Li Hung Chang is a writer who uses an axe on any man who dares Blue Pencil his Stuff.*'

"The newspaper men of New York have given me such treatment that I shall never forget them. While they have not treated my visit in the severe manner of the Germans, or in the half-patronising attitude of the London and Liverpool journals, they have tried to get at the truth regarding China and the affairs of the Far East. The editorial writers have poked a little fun at our party, but at the same time the chief editors have made my visit the occasion for long and sensible editorials upon China and her people. For this I thank them. The great United States has been our friend in the past — even though she shut out the emigrants — and she will be our strong friend in need some day.

"Of all the cities in the world I think New York is the worst. The worst, least suited to the life of

Li Hung Chang, I mean. Of course, they did not think of me when they were building it.

"But I should not want to live where, if an earthquake happened, ten thousand tons of stone and iron would topple over on my head. Oh, I have pains now in my head and neck from looking up! And when I was looking up, there were hundreds of thousands looking down at me — like people in crevices of great cliffs, four times higher than our tallest pagodas. Had they been enemies, how easy for one or ten of them to drop heavy boulders down into my carriage! But they were all friends, thousands upon thousands of friends of the Throne, of the Grand Ambassador and his party, and of the millions and millions of my countrymen. I know this to be so, for flags and banners and long streamers waved everywhere. Even the myriads of young folks and children waved little flags of yellow silk upon which were painted the Dragon, and beautiful women and girls cheered for China and clapped their pretty hands. It was all very pleasing, very satisfying to me and those with me, and I know the news will be told far and wide in China."

"*Later. Same night.* — The fine picture of President Cleveland, which I made him promise me in New York, was delivered by a special Government messenger this evening. Mrs. Cleveland's picture also accompanies the President's, and there is this brief but delightful inscription in her own hand:

'Joining with the President in sending photographs to the most distinguished of Chinese statesmen, I also request that assurances of my highest esteem be given Her Majesty the Empress Dowager.'

"It is told me that of all those fair women who have been mistresses of the Executive Mansion at Washington, Mrs. Cleveland is one of the most lovable. This I can readily believe, for I do not know when or where I have seen a face and form more pleasing to the eye. I would call her the Mother of Graciousness and the Sister of Heavenly Love. As the Chief Lady of the United States she is an ornament to her sex, and a glory to womankind the world over. I wish the illustrious and sacred Empress Dowager could know Mrs. Cleveland and the Czarina.

"President Cleveland could not have paid a higher compliment to royalty than he did to me and the members of our party. It was so great and affecting that I authorised C'Lung to expend fifteen hundred taels upon a message to the Throne telling of the American President's superlative compliment in coming all the way from Washington to New York to greet us. Could he have done more? No, if he had offered me the post of Secretary of State I could not have felt more highly honoured.

"I cannot compare Mr. Cleveland with any man whom I have met, unless it is with Prince Bismarck. Yet, while he appears to have the great force and will-power of the Iron Chancellor, I am sure he is not possessed of the same quick temper. Bismarck kicked one of his hounds, and slapped a lackey for letting the dog get in his way. I cannot imagine President Cleveland doing that, or getting so red in the face as Bismarck did. Still, one cannot always tell. I had a lesser wife [concubine] once, who, before she came to my house, was the personification of meekness and lovability. I almost began to believe, before marriage, that she was too mild in mind to be really human; but in six weeks she began to make my tea bitter, and to treat me as if I were the tail instead of the head of that establishment. I paid her twenty shoes of silver [perhaps about $300] and sent her away.

"This recalls some of the questions of another reporter in New York. He wanted to know how many wives I had, and after I told him I had as many as I needed, he was impertinent enough to ask how many I needed. The question did not please me, but I did not let him know it, for that would have been a satisfaction to him which I did not wish to give. And so I asked, 'How many wives have you?' He answered quickly, 'None.' 'Good,' I said, 'you look as if you might be able to take care of just that number.'

"When Mr. Cleveland and myself talked about wives and women in America and China, it was different. The President was seeking enlightenment, and so was I. He laughed heartily when I told him that if he were President of China he would have, as he has here, but one wife in full legal status; but that undoubtedly he would also possess a secondary wife in each province, or perhaps more. 'No, no,' he said, the tears of laughter running down his cheeks. 'But, come to think of it,' he continued, 'it takes a man capable of managing sixteen or eighteen Chinese women to govern one American girl.'

"I cannot pretend now to tell of all our activities in New York, with the dinners and receptions and the speeches. The Mayor presented me with the keys of the city; at least, that is what he said he was doing. The ceremony meant that I could go where I pleased, eat and purchase what I pleased, and even buy fine silks and satins, and the country would pay for it all. But, as it happened, I was n't allowed at any time to go where I pleased, nor to spend so much as a cash [about one eighth of a cent]. I saw the great Central Park, the Courts, and the Prison. There is another prison on an island in one of the big rivers that run around New York; or, rather, through New York, for the original city, built on an island, has spread out over territory in two or three provinces or states.

"A great river, as wide as ours at Hankow, bounds the city upon one side. I went up this fine stream when I was taken to visit the tomb of the great General Grant, who put down the rebellion of the Confederates as I had put down the long turmoils of the Taipings. And, strange enough, I was fighting the Taipings with Ching and Gordon in 1863 while General Grant was fighting to reach the rebel capital.

"I think, if they wanted to win, that the Confederates used poor judgment when they placed their capital so near the old capital of the country. Why, the distance is not greater than that between Shanghai and Nanking! If their army lost the battles in front of their capital, their Government must run away or fall into the hands of the other side. A Government that is running like a rabbit, or trapped like a guinea-pig, does not command much respect from its followers. I have looked at a map of the Confederacy, and I should have established the capital somewhere in Texas. It could be moved later.

"I cannot shed tears as some people do, — there are those who shed them when they break the shell of a painted egg, — but my heart was full of bitter sadness and sweet memory when I stood beside the tomb of my glorious departed friend General Grant. Of course, I was in a manner happy to think and know that I could stand at his holy grave, and speak to him in the Other Land of Blissful Longevity. It is at the grave of the departed that one's words are of most effect. The spirits linger there to listen, and when the distressed friend comes and speaks, his words are caught up and carried to the Sacred Hollow, where the Seven Springs are always flowing.

"And so I told the spirit of my departed and illustrious friend that I had come all the way from distant China to look upon his tomb as I had looked upon his face so many years ago. And it was the very truth; for while I had an official mission to perform for my Sovereign, and a message of good will to take to the Czar and to the rulers of Belgium, Germany, and the other countries, I had in my heart a loving desire to speak my inmost thoughts to the spirit of the famous American commander.

"I could not have returned satisfied to China had I left this sweet and flower-scented duty unperformed. I offered sweet incense and holy flowers to his spirit. I placed a booklet of prayers at his head, and I asked his blessed spirit to think of me always, and to give me welcome to the Land of Sunshine and Golden Hours. This done, I am filled with an ocean of peace and content; just as when, at the grave of my illustrious and most holy mother, I find joy of the heart and incense of the mind.

"I have thought and thought so much of General Grant. He came to China covered with the honour and plaudits of the whole world, and we honoured him still more; we honoured him as no foreigner before or since has been honoured in our country.

"And — is it not strange? — was he speaking to me? — of General Grant I was thinking when the Japanese ruffian attempted my life at Shimonoseki; when the Marquis Ito and myself, as representatives of our nations, were engaged in the treaty of peace. Is it not strange?

"Yes, I even looked beyond to the trees of General

Grant and Mrs. Grant, and spoke to him as I felt the burning of the maniac's bullet!"

The Viceroy's memoirs take it as being well known that during the visit of General and Mrs. Grant to the Far East the Japanese honoured them, among many ways, by the planting of two splendid trees of the Samurai clan on a little island opposite the city of Shimonoseki, dedicating the ground as sacred. Upon one tree was hung a copper portrait and inscription of the General, and a like placard with the picture of Mrs. Grant upon the other. It is recorded locally that soon after General Grant's death the tree dedicated to him withered away, but that the other grew green and luxuriant until Mrs. Grant's death, when it, too, died.

CHAPTER XIII

WHAT HE SAW IN AMERICA

"Philadelphia, the city of Brotherly Love, as it is called, also the city of the Cradle of American Liberty. I want to put down a few impressions now, for in a few days more I shall be commencing the long journey across the United States toward the Pacific Ocean and my beloved home. I am getting homesick for China; and although of late I have been sending brief despatches by cable to the Court, always with love and reverence for the illustrious Throne, I am anxious to tell China about my triumphal journey in foreign lands, as a first wife is to relate the antics of her first-born boy.

"If New York is the noisiest, most mind-distracting and elbow-rubbing place I ever saw, and Washington the most beautiful and open, — though I have no doubt my French friends would not thank me for saying this, especially considering the woods of Paris [the Viceroy probably refers to the Bois de Boulogne or the wide boulevards], — Philadelphia is one of the most smiling of cities.

"Of course, I mean the people, for I cannot say that the city has any sections which compare at all with the upper parts of New York, from Grant's tomb and beyond; nor has it anything half so impos-

ing in buildings or thoroughfares as the Capitol and
Pennsylvania Avenue of Washington.

"The crowds are not as dense as they are in New
York, nor as well-dressed as those in Washington or
Paris, but they are better-natured than any I have
seen anywhere. Clean, nice-looking people, too,
with smiles all over their faces, and cheers and
'hellos' and other friendly greetings coming from
their throats.

"I think the place well named 'City of Brotherly
Love.' But I am going to invent a new title, —
which I told the Mayor, and he said he would write
it down, — and call it the Place of a Million Smiles.
That is almost poetic, but it is proper, for I have
also written some lines on the Liberty Bell, which
are yet to be rewritten when I return to China."

Whether Li Hung Chang ever rewrote his lines
upon the Liberty Bell, composed during his stay in
Philadelphia, is not known. Certain it is that a
careful search of his quite countless manuscripts
and notes fails to reveal any further attempt to
improve or revise the few original lines, although in
several places in his memoirs of later date he refers
to the Liberty Bell and his visit to Philadelphia.

The poem to which he refers, and which has an
excellent cadence and metre according to Chinese
standards, is extremely difficult of rendition in
English, if attempt is made to follow the author's
rather involved thought: —

To my eyes they did point out the symbol of Liberty,
And to my ears they did direct the sound.
It was only a sound of dong-dong.
And it came from an instrument of brass made by man.
The bell did not ring to my ears;
I could not hear the voice in my ears;
But in my heart its tones took hold,
And I learned that its brazen tongue
Even in silence told of struggles against wrong.

These good sons of America
Call the Liberty Bell ancient;
But I who come from the oldest of the lands,
A student of the philosophy of the ages,
Know that what this bell speaks
Is of Heaven's wisdom,
Millions of centuries before the earth was born.

It repeats the heart words of the gods;
It repeats, only repeats:
But let it do so to the end.

In his prose regarding the Liberty Bell, the
Viceroy speaks again of its age, but in a much
lighter vein: —

"They showed me a beautifully-shaped old bell,
which is in Independence Hall, and is called the Bell
of Liberty; which means that at its ringing all men
within sound of its voice know they are free. But
they do not ring it any more because it is cracked.
Is Liberty cracked also?

"When I was informed that it was considered
'old,' in fact, called the 'Old Liberty Bell,' I asked
regarding its age, and some of the officials began
looking quizzically one to another. The Governor

of the State himself did not know its age, but finally some fellow with sharp eyes discerned a date on the symbol, whether inside or out I cannot say, and announced that it was some hundred or two years old.

"Ho! a hundred or two hundred (I forget which) years old! He! we should laugh in China if any one should call anything old at that age. It is simply an infant, still suckling. I laughed at the mention, and I told the Governor. He winked and said: 'Yes, Viceroy, all the nations are suckling infants compared to your venerable land.' . . . With that I bowed and thanked him, and I liked him for his speech.

"The great celebration for our party in this city was held principally about the place where the Liberty Bell is guarded — a building called Independence Hall. It is a small structure, not half as large as the Hall of Sacred Records at Canton, nor even of the Temple of the Great Philosopher at the Forbidden City. Here it was that the first Assembly of American representatives met to declare war upon England, and freedom from her heavy taxes. The English taxed everything the Americans used, almost, excepting the air and the water. The worst tax of all was upon tea grown in China. The Americans were very fond of tea, and they wanted much of it. So England decided that she could raise large revenues by taxing the tea. Then the Americans threw the tea into the harbours, tax and all, and would drink nothing but milk and water and whisky for a long time. Not much tea was drunk for eight years, when the war ended with England beaten. It was what she deserved. I should hate any man who deprived me of my sou-chong [a rare variety of tea, such as the Viceroy carried as a present to the Czar and Czarina, and such as he invariably used himself whenever it was obtainable].

"There were several speeches in and about Independence Hall, even myself making a brief address, which was translated by — I cannot recall his name, a secretary of our Washington legation. It was only a few sentences, the best wishes of the Chinese nation to the United States. I also spoke a few words in English: 'I am proud to be welcomed in the land of Washington.'

"I must not forget the Mayor of Philadelphia, the Honourable Mr. Warrick [Warwick], who was a jolly fellow, wearing a silk hat and a perpetual smile. The smile suited his city. Mr. Honourable Mayor made one of the longest speeches I have heard on this trip, and he put me to sleep. Yes, I really fell into a deep doze during his spouting, and it took roars of laughter to awaken me to the sense of my position. When I opened my eyes I saw thousands of people laughing and clapping their hands, and at first I thought it must have been some very humorous or witty remark of the speaker's that had brought about such an extraordinary outburst of good nature. Then I saw that everybody was looking at me, includ-

ing the Honourable Mayor himself. He was laughing with the rest! Of course, I felt a little embarrassed. Then the speaker said, half to me and half
to the immense audience, 'His Excellency does not
like long speeches, evidently; so I will cut mine
short.' This being translated to me I had my secretary say to the Honourable Mayor that I *did* like
long speeches, for during them I could have long
sleeps. The Honourable Mayor repeated my words
to his hearers, and there was laughter and cheer-
ing for several minutes. Anyway, the Honourable
Mayor finished what he had to say quickly, the
bands began to play, and the soldiers — they were
Pennsylvania State Troops [National Guard] —
began to march, and our party entered carriages and
were driven up to Broad Street.

"Broad Street is well named. It is very broad,
and many miles long; the longest straight street in
all the world. I looked down it both ways from the
City Hall, and it seemed to have no endings. Some
one told me it was thirty miles in length, which, if
true, is nearly one and one half times as long as the
great outer wall of Peking. In New York their principal street is called Broadway, when it is not broad
at all, but narrow, as thoroughfares go in this country. I think it is not as wide as the Hatemen Road
in Peking; but with its buildings it makes me think
of the Si-kiang River at Sin-chow, with its tremendous depths and high banks. But Broadway leads
the universe for business, and 'Business' is the key-

note of progress to-day. In America, especially, everything is 'Business,' even to the art of writing. Nobody in the United States writes for the mere love of the work. No, the most immortal poem or the greatest tale of true love and heroism must be paid for before the writers will let their manuscripts out of their hands. It is wonderful to think that if I had been paid even a tael for each full page I have written I should be almost a millionaire!"

It may be well to explain here, lest the explanation made in the introduction be already forgotten, that Li Hung Chang's favourite writing-paper — if we are to judge by what he used — was extra heavy, and cut to a size approximating a postal-card, though not of exactly that shape. His written characters were large, about a 36 point in type measurement, while his emphasised or exclamatory words or characters were often written much larger. This, being considered, with the further fact that seldom or never did he write beyond three lines to a "page," will help to render this last statement of his less exaggerated than it seems upon its face to be.

"I find that the matter of local or provincial pride is the same the world over. Londoners, in spite of the fog and damp of their great city, will tell you that it is the best place on the planet to live in. New Yorkers say that outside of New York there is little to see, and they let their local pride lead them to scoff at and make fun of Philadelphia. Of course, the intelligent people know that this is only palaver, but the ignorant get it into their heads, and wag their tongues as if it were the sacred truth.

"And this makes me think of what one of the reporters said to our party when we came from New York. He said that when we were in Philadelphia we would be either dead or asleep. I did not make reply at the time, but I have since thought that there was more danger of being dead in New York, with all the rush and noise overhead and on all sides, than in Philadelphia.

"But was it not humorous that in all my travels, however tired and worn I might be, I never went to sleep in public before? I had a temptation to tell the Mayor of Philadelphia, when he and the other officials came to meet our party at a junction point [Germantown?], what the New York reporter had said, but I was afraid it might offend him, for I did not know what a good-natured man he was. Afterward he himself told me how all the country called Philadelphia slow and sleepy, so I see that I should not have hurt his feelings at all."

"*Late, same night.* — To-night I visited the Union League, and was served a delightful Chinese dinner with wines and tea from Canton. It was the best that my stomach has received since leaving home.

"A great number of prominent people were there. I have a complete list, and will preserve it. But a few I will mention now: the Honourable Governor of the State, who was also a General in the great Civil War; Mr. Wanamaker, the foremost merchant of the United States, besides several leading editors and writers, among them Mr. Smith."

"*Next morning.* — General Hastings, the Governor of this great State, called upon me this morning to bid me adieu, and to present one or two young ladies and several members of his staff. I gave the Governor a strong invitation to visit me in China, and I told him that if he would come and spend a half a year in the quiet of my home in Peking, I would make him so pleased and comfortable that he would not ever want to return to the noise of Pennsylvania. He thanked me cordially, and said he would give the matter careful thought. General Stewart, who was with the Governor, asked me if I could not make him the head of my provincial army. He said he loved to fight. 'In that case, General,' I said to him, 'we do not want you, for armies that are always looking for battle usually get more than they bargain for.'

"I am sure that Governor Hastings is by far the handsomest man I have seen in all these Western countries. He ought to hold the position of emperor or king, or at least be duke of a duchy. It was a pity that he did not appear in uniform, for he is a born general-in-chief in appearance, and of most commanding presence.

"When the Governor stood near me I was not so large as before, for I had to look up at a slant into his eyes. I asked him how tall he was, and what he weighed without his clothes on, and he told me; but I have forgotten the figures just now. At any rate at the Union League we stood back to back, and he was an inch and two thirds taller than myself. Together we were the biggest pair of men in the club.

"I had several delicious American drinks called 'cocktails,' and I asked Salang to find out just what ingredients were used, and how they were made. There was just enough spice and sweetness to them to suit my taste, and I do not think they would hurt me if taken not too frequently.

"I feel that I shall sleep most calmly to-night."

After the above no entry appears to have been made for a week or ten days; for as Western dates or places are seldom given, and Chinese dates, when used, appear to be the markings of time in a number of different epochs, it is next to impossible to know with any degree of certainty where the following lines were written; but, presumably, from the general tone, they were written west of the Rocky Mountains: —

"*After three days on the train.* — Again I must think of Russia with its vast plains and heaven-reaching mountains. But here the parallel of thought must end; for with Russia all the wild and newer country is far to the east, while in the United States it is the west that is widespreading and new. Yet I must not be misunderstood, nor must I leave in my records statements that I myself will take wrongly in the times to come when facts, figures, and impressions are not as plain as they are to-day.

"In this wonderful Western empire of the American Union there is the same spirit of enterprise and business, with all modern progress, that there is along the seaboard of the Atlantic. And to think that fifty years ago there was not a settlement of stationary people in the hundreds of miles we have been travelling since we left the great river of America, the Mississippi.

"Can it be true? Can it be that all these changes have taken place since I took my examinations for the Han-lin? It must be, for I have heard it from every one, and a whole nation cannot lie.

"For hours and hours we travel, and see nothing but great ranches with cattle, or vast stretches of country without a living man or woman or fowl. Then there will be a small town, then another, then another; until finally the train rushes through the outskirts of a big city, and into a station that makes one think again of New York, Chicago, or London. And there are high buildings everywhere, so high that men look like children when seen from their roofs. Heaven help this country whenever an earthquake comes!

"I cannot see, in spite of the explanations that have been made to me, what is gained by having these structures built up so that they almost stop the clouds going by. Yes, I can see in New York, for New York is built upon an island, and the shippers and others do not want to go across rivers and bays to do their business. The city becomes crowded, and land is so valuable that those who own it send their edifices up into the air, which is free to use as high as they want to go. Yes, I can understand New York's 'cloud-stoppers'; but I cannot understand why these Western cities, with cheap land for hundreds of miles in all directions, will try to see how many great buildings they can crowd together in one place. Still, I suppose if I should write a whole volume, and make a present of it for circulation among the business men of these cities, they would not even thank me for my meddling. Anyway, it is none of my concern; and, besides, I do not expect to see the places again.

"I care nothing for mere places, unless there is some charm of the mind or heart to draw and hold me. And no place because of itself can have a claim upon my affections. There must be some human or ancestral association connected with a place if I am to think about it, or dream about it, or write about it.

"Moscow as Moscow is nothing to me; but as the place where I witnessed such overpowering ceremonials, where I saw the Czarina, and where I presented to her the Sacred Ring, sent by the illustrious and ever virtuous Empress Dowager, it is a place enshrined deep in my heart.

"And so with Essen — I hate its smoke and heat, but I love Essen because of Herr Krupp, and admire Essen because of her cannons.

"And so with Hawarden.

"And so with Philadelphia and Washington and Mt. Vernon.

"And so with home — where our loved ones are! 'T was an American that wrote a great sweet song of home. I know the air, for I heard the bands play it on the warships when I was a young man, but I do not know the words as they were written. However, the words are in the heart of each human being — just as the *dong-dong-dong* of the Old Liberty Bell at Philadelphia is in the national hearts of all men, before those hearts are turned to something else by pride or selfishness or greed of gain and power."

The great Viceroy wrote but little more of his memoirs while on American soil. What he did write was by way of advice to his countrymen in the United States, that they should obey the laws faithfully, and live in peace and concord with the people about them, save their money, and eventually return to the land of their ancestors.

His last paragraphs, written at San Francisco, the day before his sailing for China, are as follows: —

"To-day my friends took me far out toward the Golden Gate, and gave me my first view of the broad Pacific from this side of the world.

"I could not believe it was so many thousand miles across. For as I stood there upon those high cliffs at one side of the narrow entrance to the great bay of San Francisco, I strained my tired eyes across the waters, and I thought I could see in the beautiful distance the holy mirage of my native land. Those about me talked and pointed; but I heeded them not — for my very soul was reaching out to the souls of China. I saw the Throne, and I bowed my knee to Their Illustrious Majesties. I saw Tientsin and Canton and Hankow — all places I love and shall ever love.

"Returning to my apartments, I had nothing more to say. I have seen the world in these months. Now all I ask is the supreme joy of kissing the earth of my native land."

CHAPTER XIV

SHORT NOTES FROM HIS DIARY

"*July* 10, 1899. — The Empress Dowager calls, with an attempt at humour, the T'wan-lien [provincial militia] a 'tiger ride,' because it has got into the control of the Great Sword Society. Perhaps Her Majesty will yet learn that such animals and such riders, when half encouraged, devour their friends as well as their enemies."

"*Nanking*, 1869. — All foreigners regard China in the light of a yellow corpse, buried by itself, and never to awaken without the white devil's medicines. When they are looking upon China these foreigners all use the same spectacles; yet at home they fight among themselves, and have more bitter hatreds against each other than they have against us. The French hate the Germans, and the Russians kill the Jews, but they are all Christians when they come to China."

"*Peking*, 1900. — How idle is much of this talk that we hear about overthrowing the Dynasty, and substituting a Chinese family to reign in place of the Manchus! Every one knows, including myself, that there is no Chinese family sufficiently respected to rule this country in peace and order."

(Without date.) — "Kang Yu-wei is sometimes a patriotic official, sometimes a foolish meddler, and oftentimes a brainless ass."

"*Suchau, August,* 1864. — If the Taipings had a little generalship to go along with their wild fanaticism, they would have marched north and driven the Imperial family from Peking. For some time it appeared as if the new so-called Emperor Tien-teh [Hung Siu-tsuen] would really establish a dynasty, and rule the whole Middle Kingdom. But he was only an impostor in religious matters, a fakir among the people, and in no sense a military leader. It is true that he had a number of brilliant lieutenants among the Wangs; but these men, even, came under his unholy spell, and were handicapped in their plans and movements."

"*December,* 1898. — Whenever there is trouble I am sent as a doctor, yet whether the patient dies or gets suddenly well I receive no credit, but always blame. Whether it is the seizing of Kiao-chow by the Germans, the demanding of Wei-hai-wei by the British, or the bursting of the Yellow River banks, I am always the physician in attendance; but, instead of collecting a fee, I am usually subject to a fine for my trouble and skill.

"And now with the present affair in Shantung, Chang Ju-mei [the Governor] and myself receive all the blame, and are denounced on all hands. Of course the excuse for this is that we have not dealt properly with the finances of the river improvements, but the real reason is that Chang Ju-mei and myself are unutterably opposed to the Big Swords being allowed to meet and organise. They mean nothing good but much harm, yet the Government will not consent to their suppression. For his share in combating their growth Governor Chang has lost his position, and the hot-headed Yu Hsien, Treasurer of the Hu-nan and Tartar General at Nanking, has been sent in his place. Now this very appointment indicates just how the Court feels toward these organised ruffians who called themselves patriots and defenders of the State, for Yu Hsien is one of the most bigoted of officials, and has in the past allowed battles to be fought against the missionaries and converts, especially the Roman Catholics. Perhaps our Government is willing that more parts of the empire be grabbed by foreign nations on account of these fellows."

In 1886 the Viceroy first mentions Yuan Shih-k'ai: "Yuan Shih-k'ai is one of the bravest of our men, and an excellent soldier. In 1884 he was not afraid to stand up to the Japanese in Korea, and it is regrettable that he did not have a large force under his command. Had he been possessed of two or three army corps, the story of the war I believe would have been very different. He is a great admirer of the Germans, especially of their military system.

Of course this is natural, for many of his troops were German trained, and he did not leave them behind when he was appointed Governor of Shantung."

"*Peking, October 20,* 1900. — To-day I had a long conference with Sir Claude Macdonald, one of the brightest and best diplomats Great Britain has ever sent to China. Sir Claude and myself have always been on the closest of terms, and are true personal friends, although at times we do not admire each other in foreign office affairs. The same could be said of Sir Nicholas O'Conor, the diplomat who could make more friends for England than any minister I ever knew."

(Without date.) — "It is indeed a good thing for the country that Prince Ching held back his Manchu troops during the siege of the Legations. I saw him to-day, and we have become better friends than ever before. He told me that during July Prince Tuan kept urging him to make an attack, insanely telling him that if the Ministers and their friends were once slaughtered to the last person the Powers would never dare to send representatives to China again. Oh, what an insane and contemptible idea! Ching knew, as he said, that such an act would be unforgivable by the Powers, and that if necessary a million men would be sent to China to compel reparation and seek revenge. Ching declares also that it was all he could do to keep his troops in check, for the ferocious spirit of the Boxers had entered the hearts of officers and men, and all of them thirsted for the blood of the foreigners and native converts.

"After my talk with Prince Ching I called at the American Legation, and had a good visit with my friend Major Conger. I told him what I had learned from Prince Ching, without that black part relating to Tuan; and he said that he knew that the foreigners who lived through the terrible eight weeks of the siege could and did thank Prince Ching that they were alive when the allies came to the relief.

"As it was, China was disgraced in the eyes of civilisation, and the whole nation was humiliated and scorned; but if Ching had been a weaker man, and had given way either to the commands or the importunities of the Empress Dowager and Prince Tuan, that surrender on his part would have been the vital step in the obliteration of the Chinese Empire from the political map of the world. I hated Ching for the words he uttered when I went to Japan, but I have forgiven him with all my heart, and gladly bow to him as the saviour of his country."

(Without date.) — "I have written —— that during my many years' experience with foreigners in the conduct of business I have become thoroughly familiar with their characters, and I have found that, no matter what they are engaged in, they act honourably, without deceit or falsehood."

"*April*, 1898. — It does not matter what my enemies may accuse me of; in all my life I have been on the side of law and order, and I have never enquired whether those twin institutions were white or yellow. Decency is like gold, the same in all countries."

"*June* 11, 1887. — England has ever asserted that in all my diplomatic work I have had Russia's interests constantly in view. England is very wrong, just as she has been many times before in other matters. If I have appeared to work for Russia's interest, it is because in so doing I have believed that I was accomplishing the greatest good for China. The British Foreign Office caused me to be berated officially and through the Press over the Manchurian agreement with the Czar's Government; but the British refused to say that they would help us in the slightest during our Japanese conflict or after; while Russia, at the close of the war at least, let Japan understand that China was not alone."

(Without date.) — "Bishop Favier, if I am ever the sovereign of a nation, and you are without a position — though men of your calibre are rare — I will offer you the place of generalissimo of the forces! You are a noble soldier, Favier, and you saved the lives of your little army. I hope the head of your sect [the Pope] will make of you the head of the Church."

The Viceroy alludes to the remarkable and heroic defence of the new French Cathedral made by Bishop Favier with a few French, Belgian, and German marines, and his three thousand converts. Though attacked for days and nights at a time, the Bishop and his band nobly defended their position, inflicting great loss upon the Boxer hordes which assailed the church.

"*Written in Canton, in early March*, 1900. — There can be little doubt but the southern viceroys have received orders to be prepared to despatch all foreigners. Who is responsible for such dastardly commands? How well the authors knew better than to send such outrageous documents to me!"

(Without date.) — "Foreign Governments say they lease our lands. We know they are gone forever."

(Without date.) — "Sometimes the pretensions of these 'learned men' from the West anger me, at other times I feel sorry for them, and now very often I sit down and laugh at them until my dinner is all upside-down! To-day I was talking with a 'Professor,' who came all the way from Massachusetts to teach in the new University, and he was telling me that he should be lost until his books arrived.

"'I have eighteen large volumes that I use in my work,' he said; 'books of science, art, ethics, and lexicography.'

"'Eighteen?' I asked. 'Do you need them all?'

"'Oh, yes; but they cover the whole range of my work.'

"I did not like to smile in his face, but I could not help it. He asked me the reason for my apparent merriment.

"'I was only thinking of how much more exhaustive your Western wisdom must be than ours,' I replied. Then I told him that King He, our literary Emperor, had compiled and issued the Pei Wan Yun Fu [Dictionary] in 1711, and that it consisted of one hundred and thirty volumes!"

(Without date.) — "How splendid a thing it would be if our ancient motto 'King sik tsze chil' [Reverence the written word and keep it holy] could be hung conspicuously on the walls of the various foreign offices!"

CHAPTER XV

ACCORDING to his memoirs, Li Hung Chang, then Governor of the two Kwang provinces, foresaw in the early part of 1900 that China would shortly be embroiled with foreign nations over the Boxers, or Great Sword Society, who were becoming aggressive in the north. In February of that year this entry is found in his diary: —

"For the third time I have memorialised the Throne to trample under foot the I-h o-k'uan [Patriotic Peace Fists], but as no action was taken upon my former memorials to put an end to this organisation of ruffians and hard-hitters, I expect but little attention will be paid to my later petition. I have tried time and again, almost without number, to impress the Throne with the idea that China has nothing to gain and everything to lose by opposing the so-called foreign devils. It would be utterly impossible to drive them out; and last, but most important, our country would be poorer in many ways if the foreigners ever withdrew, willingly or otherwise.

"During my last days at the capital I made every effort to impress the truth of these views upon the Court. The Empress is apparently in sympathy with these sentiments, and Jung-lu [one of the most influential and intimate counsellors of the Dowager] is really a strong and abiding friend of the Christians. But Prince Tuan secretly favours the Patriotic Peace Fists — as I am personally aware — and will use every means he can to persuade Their Majesties that the society can exterminate the foreigners if it is not interfered with. Tuan has a powerful following; but I fear most of all that Tze Hsi believes what he says, and secretly favours the Great Swords."

In April, 1900, the Viceroy makes this observation: —

"I have received from the Throne the following letter, which I am candid enough to believe is but for effect abroad: 'The establishment by the rural population in each province of militia for their own protection, and for the preservation of their lives and families, is at bottom simply the good old ancestral practice of keeping a lookout and lending mutual assistance; and so long as those concerned mind their own business, there is no reason why they should be interfered with. All that is to be feared is that amongst such persons the good and bad may get mixed, and that pretexts may be taken to raise trouble with native Christians. It must be remembered that the Sovereign regards all with equal benevolence, without distinction of territorial division, for which reason the populations concerned should obey the spirit of this idea, and refrain from giving vent to their private resentments, in such wise as to cause hostility and render themselves liable to punishment. Let us tell Your Excellency that we expect the governors-general and governors concerned to give strict directions to local authorities, to issue plain-speaking proclamations as occasion may require, calling upon all persons to attend to their own affairs, and always to keep on peaceful terms with others, not ignoring the spirit of these earnest exhortations.'"

The Viceroy comments: "This is all nonsense; it means nothing right. I know the country will now get into trouble over these ruffians. But they are not numerous in my provinces, and dare not show their heads."

He writes (supposedly in May, 1900): —
"Hurried telegrams from the Throne have come to me, urging that I suppress any lawlessness in my territory. This angers me, for it is but a blind and subterfuge. There is no lawlessness here! and there will be none!

"I have sent messages every day of late to Jung-lu, urging him to employ all means in his power to win the Empress Dowager strongly over to the side of the foreigners. She is wavering, for she wants to believe what both of her strongest admirers say; while these two men [Jung-lu and Prince Tuan] are on diametrically opposite sides."

"Oh, I am sorry for China! If the Legations are

disturbed, the foreign nations will march through the land with fire and sword. Even the United States, our friend heretofore, will send her armies and fleets against us."

"*Later* [without date]. — The final blow has been struck by these wretches of the Patriotic Peace Fists, with the killing of the German Minister, Von Ketteler, whom I knew and whom I first met in Germany. What will become of China now? Still, Heaven is aware that I have urged and urged against the bandits until I am weary! Prince Tuan, who was born a hater of the Christians, and has grown more hateful with his years, has probably convinced the Throne that if the Boxers are not interfered with they will clean the land of all foreigners. What hellish rubbish! His ignorance must be paid for by his country."

Though it is evident that Li was deeply aroused over the troubles at the north, he seems to have been sufficiently at peace with himself to conduct an ancient ceremony at Canton, for the next entry in his notes reads: —

"To-day we performed the full ceremony of the Tilling of the Soil. All my officials and myself, in full court dress, went by chair to the Temple of Shen Nung, beyond the East Gate, and performed our obligations. The great and illustrious Shen Nung is the Divine Husbandman who reigned 4700 years ago. It was he who invented agriculture, and to him the world owes the most sublime reverence and respect."

Some time later he writes: "It is as I expected: there is war in the north, and Tuan has treacherously persuaded the Throne to let the Imperial troops join with the Boxers in an attempt to exterminate the foreigners. My heart is sick — I wash my hands of the whole affair."

He next writes at Tientsin (presumably late in August): "Here I am once more in the same old house I occupied for so long, and where I spent so many happy days and nights — and unhappy ones, too, I may add; for to be Viceroy of Chihli, and Grand Secretary at the same time, brought many cares and troubles to my mind. Yet all the difficulties were surmounted and many good things accomplished; therefore, as the sum total, I was happy and satisfied.

"Now, my great task — perhaps the last great task of my career — is to save China. Their Majesties are in temporary exile, and the foreigners are in control of the Capital. I am glad to think that many of the miscreants who got our country into this terrible fix are themselves in trouble, and will be brought to book. I do not glory in the death of any man, but there are some heads I shall be glad to see chopped off. One man in particular [the Viceroy refers undoubtedly to Prince Tuan] deserves fully, if any man ever did, the ling-chi [the death of a thousand cuts]. I hope it will be the reward of his damnable meddling.

"All the foreign nations are against us, it would seem. No, there is an exception, and the exception may prove our salvation from being sliced up like a water-melon. The Americans are, of course, acting with France, Russia, England, Germany, and Japan, but at the same time I have received assurances from the American commander and from the Washington Government that the United States will oppose morally and physically, if necessary, the partition of China.

"My greatest fear now is from the Germans and Russians. The Germans, because of the death of their Minister, are despatching regiments every day for China, and are sending one of their greatest field marshals to command their troops. If they establish a big army in the Capital, and demand an indemnity such as they did of the French, and stay until it is paid, I fear they will never leave us. The Russians, too, have a tremendous force in Manchuria, and along the Siberian Railway; and if there is an agreement between them it may take more than a combination of the other Powers to make them relent. My hope, however, is centred in the attitude of the United States."

"*Later, same.* — Cable despatches from our Minister at Washington are reassuring. The American Government is confident that its note to the other Powers, proposing a joint indemnity to be agreed upon by myself, acting for China, and the foreign representatives, will meet with the approval of the foreign offices. Good!"

"*October* 12, *Peking*. — I have learned from a source that is beyond questioning that the Powers had determined immediately after the capture of the city to make a division of China between them. Yet it seems that, like so many dogs over the carcass of a beast, they could not agree upon their respective shares. It was determined that the European nations and Japan should act in concert, ignoring the United States. This, however, was not found to be feasible, for first England, and then Japan, weakened. The trouble is that Japan wanted that part of China as her sphere of influence which Russia claimed as her own. Perhaps amidst the quarrelling of the wolves the sheep will get away."

"*October* 15. — I visited the Russian Legation to-day, and had a meeting with the foreign ministers. The position taken in this matter by the American nation means the integrity of China. The United States has won over the other Powers to her way of thinking. Thanks be to the spirits of our fathers, our country may yet be saved from slicing. But the indemnity will be great. Yet our country will be left to us, and we can pay it. Japan, for an old enemy, is acting most fair, and it is my belief that there is a perfect understanding between Tokio and Washington."

"*Peking, at U.S. Legation, October* 19. — To-day I received an American newspaper man, and gave him a lengthy interview. I should not have talked at all with him, but for two things: his paper, which is one of great influence at Washington, has been China's advocate in all this miserable affair; and, secondly, he told me that he tried to get an interview with me at the Philadelphia junction [Germantown], but failed. So I made it up with him, and sent the thanks of China and myself to those fair-dealing people who live in the land of Lincoln and Grant and McKinley."

The American newspaper man referred to in this paragraph of the Viceroy's memoirs is the editor of the present work.

CHAPTER XVI

CALLED TO THE THRONE'S AID

BECAUSE of his well-known tendencies in favour of the foreigner, tendencies which made him a "thorn in the flesh" of the reactionaries, who were in almost undisputed control of the Peking Government, and who were responsible for the *coup d'état* of 1898, by which the Empress Dowager resumed the active throne, and the young Emperor Kuang Su was committed to a palace prison, it was desired by those in power that Li Hung Chang be induced to quit the Capital; and so, late in 1899, he was sent for by Hze Tsi, and asked to name what office outside the Capital he would consider most to his liking.

He wrote on December 12, at two o'clock A.M.:—
"Within the hour I have returned from an unpublished audience with old Buddha [the Empress Dowager], and I am ill at ease, for Her Majesty intended that I should go south, intimating that affairs were such in that quarter that I was needed there. I did not dare tell her so outright, but all this is the merest subterfuge, for while I may count my best friends right here in Peking, these very people are desirous that I be away in case of serious disturbances. Serious disturbances! Indeed, if there are such they will be of their own making and

desiring — and against wishes of mine which are well understood.

"I am an aged man now, nearing my seventy-seventh year, and perhaps they think my mental vision is dimmed so that I cannot see the real trend of affairs. It is known to the Court, and to the Grand Council, and to all who are conversant with my life that I am not seeking active office at this time. No one is better aware of this than Her Majesty, yet she pretends to think she would be honouring me further by sending me south.

"However, I will utter no further protest against this wicked policy, which, if pursued to its logical conclusion, can have but one end: the disastrous wrecking of the country and the humiliation of the Throne, if not the complete abolition of the Dynasty. I shall make a final appeal to Jung-lu, to Yuan Shih-k'ai, and even to the impetuous and calamity-seeking Prince Tuan. If this is without the desired effect, once more on my old knees I will ask Her Majesty, for the good of herself and her people, to drive the Boxer influence from the palace. But I fear Tuan has her ear, and that she is already convinced that all the foreigners will be driven into the ocean. Oh, if these great personages could have but seen the armies and navies I saw, and the giant strength of Europe and America, they would no more dream as children!"

The memoirs of the aged Viceroy do not disclose

whether he ever made these final appeals to the Powers within the Forbidden City, to the end that the complications he so plainly saw might be averted, nor do the official records indicate that he memorialised the Throne upon this subject. His diary does contain, however, a number of very brief references to his contemplated departure for the south, the last one of which reads:—

"I am being sent away from the trouble which is sure to descend upon this capital, and I am bidding good-bye to many friends as though something told me I should not see them again. As I was given my choice, I have chosen the Canton Viceroyalty."

"*My old Palace, Canton, March* 11, 1900. — My old-time friend Wu Ting Fang writes me the most earnest letter I have seen for years, a communication full of wisdom and high patriotism. I am making copies of it, and will send them as fast as I can to a number of leading spirits in the north, hoping that Dr. Wu's strong and sensible words will be followed. Our excellent Minister knows to a dot how the Government at Washington feels, and the general trend of American opinion, and it will be well for Prince Tuan and others to heed his warning."

"*March* 17. — A letter from Bishop Favier says that all friends of enlightenment at the Capital believe it was a mistake for me to leave it. I am agreeable to this opinion, but this last mistake is only one of many that I have made in life under duress."

"*March* 26. — I am sorry that when I made the
Treaty of Peace with Japan in 1895, I did not agree
to let them have the Province of Shantung along
with the other concessions; for then China would be
rid of this turbulent territory where these fanatical
Big Fists are bred like rats on a grain ship. It was
there that Yu Hsien, he of the Manchus, and an
alleged friend of the Dynasty, put swords into
their hands and greater ferocity into their hearts.
If it were mine to say — as it is Jung-lu's now — I
should soon finish Governor Yu for the ignoble part
he has played up to this time. I well know personally the ignorant and fire-eating Yu, and I would
not let him assist in the carrying of my chair."

"*March* 27. — Reports from all the northeast
country indicate that the Boxers are everywhere
rising and committing depredations. Paoting-fu,
Tientsin, and many of the smaller heins are threatened by them, and Peking itself is trembling. I can
do nothing more. It shall be my attempt from this
time on to write much and sleep more. I have spent
many sleepless hours since my arrival here. But the
time is not very remote when I shall sleep undisturbed through the ages."

"*March* 29. — A telegram from Jung-lu says the
old Buddha is completely in sympathy with the
Boxer movement, but will not consent to turn over
any Government arms to them. I credit only the
first part of his despatch."

"*April* 5. — It is regrettable that such a man as Yuan Shih-k'ai should listen to the song of anarchy that is being sung by the Boxer ruffians, as I understand he is doing. He has wide experience, and in Korea showed himself an able man and a high-minded patriot.

"But he seems to be carried away by the wild clamour of the hour, when he should know that the foreigners, even the Germans alone, are able to lay waste the entire kingdom if they but take the notion. He does not reply to my communications; therefore I shall not trouble myself to address him again. With Jung-lu it is different; he will always write in answer, though it is never possible to tell by his words just what he means. I think that he realises the complete ascendancy of Tuan over Her Majesty, and is fearful of getting himself into disfavour."

"*April* 5. — It is now high time that the authorities patch up things before the rain comes, and diminish the fuel before the fire rages."

"*April* 7. — I have written Major Conger that he had better send warning to the United States Government of approaching trouble, and then leave Peking with his family. I have the highest respect for this fine diplomat, who is a most worthy representative of a worthy people."

"*April* 16. — Perhaps, after all, the Empress

Dowager is the best personal friend I have in the world outside my own family and domicile. This I say because, with the reports coming in from all quarters that the so-called Patriotic Peace Fists [Boxers] are everywhere committing crimes against the foreigners, their persons, and their properties, I could not remain inactive or silent if I were in Peking; and that would mean that Prince Tuan would see to it that I was put out of the way. Still, to cut short this life of mine a year or two would do no great harm, unless it might be to make Lady Li a widow ahead of season. But, regardless of consequences, I should prove that in my later days I was as true to my country as I was thirty or forty years ago in the hard, long, and discouraging battles with the Taiping hordes that hoped to overthrow the empire. Nevertheless, the Long-Haired Rebels were not greater enemies of the State than some of the oily-tongued, richly-robed counsellors at this very moment basking in the smiles and confidence of Her Majesty beneath the palace roofs.

"No, I did not write in this manner while I was at the Northern Capital, and I did not utter such words, but I spoke plainly to all who had a right to listen; and if my advice is already forgotten — as it went unheeded — it will not be many moons before it is recalled again, perhaps in bitterness and sorrow.

"However, I must call a halt to myself in all this matter. My hand shakes like that of a fever patient, and my tired eyes are as those of a mummy, glazed with varnish; for I do not sleep one twelfth of each day, and my household declares that never before have I acted the double part of tyrant and ass. Yes, I am both; but in the future I shall endeavour to mend all my ways. Only this: I hope and pray that seven times seven scourges and torments will fall upon the heads of the Patriotic Peace Fists!"

"*June* 10. — I do not like the news from the north. A telegram from Shan, which I asked him to send, indicates that already in Peking the destruction of foreign property has begun. I presume some of my own buildings, leased by foreign firms, will not be spared. Anyway, I do not care. I only regret that there are so many English, German, and Japanese business places in the city."

"*June* 14. — And so the wild ruffians have killed the Chancellor of the Japanese Legation. This means war with Japan, at least. Some one else will have to go as peace commissioner, for I am done with making apologies, and then standing about while brickbats of abuse and contumely are hurled at my head."

"*June* 15. — Prince Tuan is surely in command of affairs at the Northern Capital, and leading the Throne on to sure destruction. He should hide his head in shame, a head that is filled with a mere molten slush of hatred, and is devoid of real brains.

If I were now in Peking I would brand him as the worst enemy of China in all her history. It would cost me my head to speak this way, but the satisfaction of telling the truth to the arrogant and ignorant Tuan would be worth the loss by decapitation."

"*Midnight.* — My wife declares that I will become insane over these national troubles. She is wrong, just as she often is. I should go insane if I had nothing to bother me. My normal mental state for half a century has been that of perturbation. Perhaps it is well that the Patriotic Peace Fists are giving me something to worry over, thus keeping my mind in its normal state."

"*June 22.* — A telegraphic message tells me of the outrageous killing of the German Minister! In the name of hell and purgatory and all the black valleys, what are the national miscreants thinking about? Oh, they call their leader the great Jade Emperor, and they make offerings to him, but I hope he will smite their twisted heads!

"Now it will not only be war with Japan but with the German Empire. Indeed, the Boxers have gone so far that they have committed the Throne to their conduct, and the Government of China will be held in strict accountability to the Powers. The whole Christian world will unite against us, and reach for the neck of China as a farmer grabs the feast-goose in the pen.

"All my warnings have been and are in vain. All my words have gone for naught, and the Dynasty is forever doomed. I saw the trend of events, but in my most hopeless hours I could not foresee that the ambassadorial officers of the Powers would not be safe within their own compounds. Tuan will say that these outrages were not committed by Imperial troops, and that, according to my reports, is true. But this will by no means relieve the Government of responsibility in the eyes of the outside nations. Japan is undoubtedly this minute rejoicing because of the death of her Legation Chancellor. It is the excuse they have long awaited, burning under their chagrin and disappointment, since their undeserved fruits of the war with China were taken from them. And Germany will take no apology for the murder of her Minister! If she took Kiao-chow from us for the lives of two missionaries, what will she demand for the life of Baron von Ketteler? I tremble for the consequences of all this folly!

"I did not know the Japanese official, but Baron von Ketteler was one of the last to say good-bye to me in Peking. And upon that occasion he spoke happily of our meeting in Germany four years before, when I was the guest of his own great nation. And now, my fellow-countrymen kill him in the streets of our capital! What will the Germans think now of the fine China I spoke so proudly of, and which I endeavoured to represent so worthily? And all the Christian world will more than ever look upon us as a vast aggregation of barbarians, who are not possessed of the first principles of international dealing, nor deserving of the first advances of international comity.

"I am ill."

"*June* 23. — In spite of my illness I sent urgent telegraphic messages to Prince Tuan, Jung-lu, and Yuan Shih-k'ai, telling them if they would save the nation from being sliced like a watermelon by the foreigners, they must turn all the strength of the Throne against the ruffian society. I sent also a long despatch to Prince Ching. He does not admire me much since the Japanese war, but he is a strong, sensible patriot, and undoubtedly sees the terrible chasm into which the country is likely to fall."

"*June* 24. — Sing brings me news from the city that a telegraphic despatch to the press says the Boxers are in complete control of Peking, but that Prince Ching has refused to join them with his troops. If he would but fight them with his Manchu warriors, he would save the situation. I am ill and weak."

"*June* 25. — There is an unconfirmed report in the city that the Tsung Li Yamen has sent word to the Legations that a state of war exists since the firing upon the Taku forts. If this is true, then the Government is irrevocably committed to its own destruction. I can scarcely believe that such a height of political insanity has been reached by the Court."

"*June* 29. — To-day I received from the north a copy of an edict in the name of the Emperor, but written, I know, by Her Majesty: —

"'Ever since the foundation of the Dynasty, foreigners coming to China have been kindly treated. In the reign of Tao-Kuang and Hein Fung they were allowed to trade and to propagate their religion. At first they were amenable to Chinese control, but for the past thirty years they have taken advantage of our forbearance to encroach upon our territory, to trample on the Chinese people, and to absorb the wealth of the empire. Every concession made seems only to increase their insolence. They oppress our peaceful subjects, and insult our gods and sages, exciting burning indignation among the people. Hence the burning of chapels and the slaughter of converts by the patriotic braves. The throne was desirous to avoid war, and issued edicts enjoining protection of legations and pity toward converts, declaring Boxers and converts to be equally the children of the State. With tears have we announced in our ancestral shrines the outbreak of war. Better it is to do our utmost and enter on the struggle than to seek self-preservation involving eternal disgrace. All our officials, high and low, are of one mind. There have also assembled, without official summons, several thousands of soldiers. Even children carry spears in the defence of their country.'"

"*July* 12. — After nine days in bed with little sleep and less food, I am aroused by a report which is repeated in the city, saying that I have been reappointed to the Chihli Viceroyalty. This cannot be true, for several reasons. Anyway, I shall stay where I am, in office or out. Almost to repeat the unkind words said to me fifteen years ago [Li refers to Prince Ching's remark when the former started for Japan as Peace Envoy]: 'They have started the trouble, now let them finish it.'"

"*July* 13. — The local press publishes papers confirmatory of the report that I have been named Viceroy of Chihli. I am not well enough to go north. I shall not go. That part is settled."

"*July* 14. — My entire household is in tears, because the report of my appointment is confirmed in the press to-day."

"*July* 17. — The Empress Dowager's communication arrived this morning, and the dumbfounding truth is known at last. She directs that I proceed at once to the north, saying that I am urgently needed in the present great crisis. Urgently, indeed! I was not urgently needed in Peking a few short months ago, when I was virtually told that if I had any 'loyal' advice to give I might do so, but if I was opposed to the 'sacred policy' I should hold my peace. I have decided not to go, even though it may cost me much to remain."

"*Later, same day.* — I have just forwarded to Her Majesty a telegram as follows: 'Your Majesty's confidence in me is, indeed, a very great honour, and I beg to say that I am sincerely grateful, more so than I am able to express. Yet I cannot fail to recall the folly that has now suddenly destroyed that structure of reformed administration which, during my term of more than twenty years of office as Viceroy of Chihli, I was able to build up not unsuccessfully. I fear that in the present state of my mental and physical health it will be quite impossible for me to resume that difficult post. The present time of crisis requires a different and a stronger hand than mine.'"

"*Later.* — I have sent another message to Her Majesty through Yuan Shih-k'ai, asking what may be the chances for the safe escorting of the foreign ministers from Peking to Tientsin. I said also to him that he might inform Her Majesty that I would probably start north as soon as my health permits."

"*Shanghai, July 22.* — It appears that there is nothing for me to do but to obey the decree of the Throne, and again bow and scrape and apologise

to the foreigners for the murderous doings of a
class with which I am not at all in sympathy. I
had fondly thought that I was done with all this
sort of thing, but the truth seems to be that I am
face to face with difficulties and complications such
as have never confronted us before. Of course, for
these very reasons I should be the readier to take
upon my shoulders the task; but when I consider
how absolutely unnecessary all this trouble is, and
that my sincere and unselfish advice was so wholly
scorned, I have little heart for the work."

"*Shanghai, July* 23. — This message came from
the old Buddha this morning: 'Li Hung Chang is
to obey without question our earlier decree, and to
hasten to the north, regardless of other considerations. He must know that the crisis is very serious,
and that he can, therefore, offer no further valid
excuses.'"

"*Midnight, July* 23. — I have just finished a
memorial to the Throne, which I shall forward to
Yuan Shih-k'ai at the earliest hour of the morning
by swift couriers. Though lengthy, I am keeping a
copy, that at least my own children, if denied access
to the Records, will know my words: —
"'It is to be remembered that between this our
Empire of China, and the outer barbarians, hostilities have frequently occurred since the remotest
antiquity, and our national history teaches that

the best way to meet them is to determine upon
our policy only after carefully ascertaining their
strength as compared with our own. Since the
middle of the reign of Tao-Kuang, the pressure of
the barbarians on our borders has steadily increased,
and to-day we are brought to desperate straits
indeed. In 1860 they invaded the Capital, and
burned the Summer Palace; His Majesty Hsien-
Feng was forced to flee, and thus came to his death.
It is only natural that His Majesty's posterity should
long to avenge him to the end of time, and that your
subjects should continue to cherish undying hopes
of revenge. But since that time France has taken
from us Annam, the whole of that dependency being
irretrievably lost; Japan has fought us and ousted
us from Korea. Even worse disasters and loss of
territory were to follow; Germany seized Kiao-chow;
Russia followed by annexing Port Arthur and Talien-
wan; England demanded Wei-hai-wei and Kowloon,
together with the extension of the Shanghai Settlements, and the opening of new treaty ports inland;
and France made further demands for Kuang-
Chou-wan. How could we possibly maintain silence
under such grievous and repeated acts of aggression?
Craven would be the man who would not seek to
improve our defences, and shameless would be he
who did not long for the day of reckoning. I myself
have enjoyed no small favours from the Throne, and
much is expected of me by the nation. Needless for
me to say how greatly I should rejoice were it possible

for China to enter upon a glorious and triumphant war; it would be the joy of my closing days to see the barbarian nations subjugated at last in submissive allegiance, respectfully making obeisance to the Dragon Throne. Unfortunately, however, I cannot but recognise the melancholy fact that China is unequal to any such enterprise, and that our forces are in no way competent to undertake it. Looking at the question as one chiefly affecting the integrity of our empire, who would be so foolish as to cast missiles at a rat in the vicinity of a priceless piece of porcelain? It requires no augur's skill in divination to see that eggs are more easily to be cracked than stones. Let us consider one recent incident in proof of this conclusion. Recently, in the attack by some tens of thousands of Boxers and Imperial troops upon the foreign settlements at Tientsin, there were some two or three thousand soldiers to defend them; yet, after ten days of desperate fighting, only a few hundred foreigners had been slain, while no less than twenty thousand Chinese were killed and as many more wounded. Again, there are no real defences nor fortified positions in the Legations at Peking, nor are the foreign ministers and Legation staffs trained in the use of arms; nevertheless, Tung Fuhsiang's hordes have been bombarding them for more than a month, and have lost many thousands of men in the vain attempt to capture the position.

"'The fleets of the Allied Powers are now hurrying forward vast bodies of their troops; the heaviest

artillery is now being brought swiftly to our shores.
Has China the forces to meet them? Does she possess a single leader capable of resisting this invasion?
If the foreign Powers send 100,000 men they will
easily capture Peking, and Your Majesties will then
find escape impossible. You will no doubt endeavour
once more to flee to Jehol, but on this occasion you
have no commander like Sheng Pao to hold back the
enemies' forces from pursuit; or, perhaps, you may
decide to hold another Peace Conference, like that of
Shimonoseki, in 1895? But the conditions to-day
existing are in no way similar to those of that time,
when Marquis Ito was willing to meet me as your
Minister Plenipotentiary. When betrayed by the
Boxers and abandoned by all, where will Your
Majesties find a single prince, councillor, or statesman able to assist you effectively? The fortunes of
your house are being staked by a single throw; my
blood runs cold at night at the thought of events
to come. Under any enlightened sovereign these
Boxers, with their ridiculous claims of supernatural
powers, would most assuredly have been condemned
to death long since. Is it not on record that the Han
Dynasty met its death because of its belief in magi-
cians, and in their power to confer invisibility? Was
not the Sung Dynasty destroyed because the Emperor believed ridiculous stories about supernatural
warriors clad in miraculous coats of mail?

"'I myself am nearly eighty years of age, and my
death cannot be far distant; I have received favours

at the hands of four emperors. If now I hesitate to say the things that are in my mind, how shall I face the spirits of the sacred ancestors of this Dynasty when we meet in the halls of Hades? I am compelled therefore to give utterance to this my solemn prayer, and to beseech Your Majesties to put away from you at once these vile magic workers, and to have them summarily executed.

"'You should take steps immediately to appoint a high official who shall purge the land of this villainous rabble, and who shall see to it that the foreign ministers are safely escorted to the headquarters of the Allied Armies. In spite of the heat I have hurried northwards from Canton to Shanghai, where Your Majesties' decrees urging me to come to Peking have duly reached me. Any physical weakness, however serious, would not have deterred me from obeying this summons, but perusal of your decrees has led me to the conclusion that Your Majesties have not yet adopted a policy of reason, but are still in the hands of traitors, regarding these Boxers as your dutiful subjects, with the result that unrest is spreading and alarm universal. Moreover, I am here in Shanghai without a single soldier at my command, and even should I proceed in all haste in the endeavour to present myself at your palace gates, I should meet with innumerable dangers by the way, and the end of my journey would most probably be that I should provide your rebellious and turbulent subjects with one more carcass to hack into mince-

meat. I shall therefore continue in residence here for
the present, considering ways and means for raising
a military force and for furnishing supplies, as well
as availing myself of the opportunity of ascertaining
the enemies' plans, and making such diplomatic sug-
gestions as occur to me to be useful. As soon as my
plans are complete I shall proceed northwards with
all possible speed.'"

During the following weeks the aged Viceroy wrote
but little in his diary, for physical ills sorely beset
him; and at the same time he was unwilling to proceed to the north until given assurances by the
Government not only that the persons and properties of the foreigners in Peking would be given the
fullest protection and security from that time forth,
but that those who were responsible for the outbreak
would be summarily and adequately punished.

"*August 2.* — I think too much of my good name
to have it associated with those of the inciters in this
outrageous matter. I will not go north until certain
promises I have asked for are made by Her Majesty
and those about her."

"*August 8.* — A sick man has been appointed
Peace Plenipotentiary to treat with the Powers.
How can I hold my head up and demand consideration in this matter when my limbs are almost too
weak to support my body?"

The last lines in Li's diary in relation to the Boxer outbreak appear to have been written at Tientsin on August 18: —

"A rest of a few days, and then I will proceed to Peking to stay the hand of the Powers as much as in me lies. Oh, if my own hand were not so weak, and my cause so much weaker! The Court is in hiding, and the people are distracted. There is no Government, and chaos reigns. I fear the task before me is too great for my strength of body, though I would do one thing more before I call the earthly battle over. I would have the foreigners believe in us once more, and not deprive China of her national life; and I should like to bring old Buddha back to the palace, and ask her if she had learned a lesson."

The "Grand Old Man of China" indeed did accomplish the restoration of China in his long-drawn-out negotiations with the representatives of the ten foreign Powers directly interested, and on every side it was admitted that in his seventy-ninth year the one-time wisher for the poet-laureateship of China had at least won the freshest and greenest laurel wreath among her statesmen and diplomats of all time.

But the ill and aged Peace Plenipotentiary was not to be granted the wish that he might again see the Empress Dowager face to face in the palace. Though she had undoubtedly "learned a lesson," it was not to be Li Hung Chang's privilege and pleasure to ask her if she had; for while the old Buddha, as she was familiarly and endearingly called by those who knew her best, was on her return journey to Peking, ten months after her unceremonious flight from the Forbidden City, his last illness came upon the famous Viceroy, and his death occurred on 7th November, 1901, at his Peking residence, Tze Hsi arriving at her capital on 6th January following.

CHAPTER XVII

HIS FIGHT TO HOLD KOREA

"*March*, 1882. — It would appear as if the Palace intended to lay the entire burden of Korean troubles upon my shoulders, and I presume there is nothing for me to do but use every means in my power to balk the plain designs of the Nipponese. My reports indicate as plainly as the sun in the sky that it is the hope of the Islanders to bring affairs at Seoul to such a crisis that China will either be compelled to assert suzerainty without equivocation, or forever henceforward pretend to no claims in that quarter."

"*March* 17, 1882. — Without edict the Throne has commanded me to assume sole and complete charge of our interests in the Hermit Kingdom, and it now behoves me to prepare for such emergencies as may arise in that troubled and troublesome country. With scarcely a tribute that was worth while in all these hundreds of years, Korea has ever been independent and even resentful of our influence or interest; but just so soon as trouble looms up on the horizon, from causes having their source either within or without the kingdom, she comes begging for help. And help has never been denied, for the people of the country are our people, and they share with us the everlasting dislike for the pygmy Nipponese, with their strutting ways and ignorant presumptions. We taught the Nipponese what little they knew in the beginning, which they speedily unlearned, supplanting that knowledge with a vain assumption of superiority in most matters. They treat the Koreans as rank inferiors, and have come to believe that because of its proximity Korea is a vassal state.

"I regret to learn that the Tai Wen Kun is stirring up internal trouble at a time when he should be giving all the support of which he is capable to his son, and thus more effectually circumventing the machinations of the Mikado's agents. I must see to it that Li Hsia Ying [the Tai Wen Kun, or Chief Court Lord] is communicated with at once, to the end that he will not bring disagreeable matters to a head too soon.

"The Imperial Resident [at Seoul, Yuan Shih-k'ai] sends by special messenger for instructions as to what it is best to do in the event of a renewed outbreak against the Japanese. The details of the former outbreak have not yet been reported to me, and I am quite in the dark as to how great is the damage. If I did not believe affairs would be forced to a critical point, I would order a thousand of my men to go secretly to the support of the Imperial Resident to be ready for his call."

"The Imperial Resident writes me that the Japanese Minister [Hanabusa] is doing all in his power by underhand tricks and secret games to bring about an attack upon his own legation, and that I must be prepared for an outbreak to occur at any time. Shih-k'ai declares that many Korean traitors, in the pay and service of the Mikado's agents, are ready at the word from their masters to make trouble about the Japanese legation, thereby offering an excuse for Hanabusa to appeal to the Tokio authorities."

"I have despatched one hundred and twenty of my most trusted men from Paoting-fu to report directly to the Resident and ferret out the blackguards. Mong is in command, and that alone means that the traitors will be located promptly, and their names and persons made known to the King's police. I expect excellent returns from the mission, and the Resident is to be highly commended for the thoroughness of his information."

"*August* 11, 1882. — The news from Seoul is very satisfactory, at least in one important respect, and I shall soon have as a guest an old devil I have much longed to see — dead or alive; for a courier from our strong man in Korea [Yuan Shih-k'ai] informs me that he has succeeded at last in throwing the bag over Li Hsia Ying's troublesome head, and that under proper escort he is on the way hither."

"*Later, same date.* — A second messenger from the Resident has arrived. He hurried on ahead of the Tai Wen Kun's party, and believes he is at least thirty li in advance of them. The old devil was landed at Shanghai-kwan, and is being hurried along on the lower coal road.

"If this man were not such an inborn detester of everything that pertains to Nippon or the Nipponese, I should be tempted sorely to make his head a decoration upon the Yamen walls. The Throne does not as yet, at this hour, know of the success of my plans with reference to Li Hsia Ying, but all the officials will be glad to know that he is no longer at Seoul."

"*My Bedroom.* [Without date, but probably written a few days after the foregoing.] — Even in times of stress and strife it is given to the thinking man to have moments, if not hours, during which he may retire to the company of himself, and think quietly and soberly upon what fate has done or may do for him. Oftentimes —though I have few hours which are not given to official, family, or business cares — I find excellent recreation for the mind in traversing back the years and noting their mistakes and victories, or in attempting to peer into the future, and see in the dim light of the yet-to-be what fate or the gods may have in store.

"Yesterday, upon returning from Peking, weary of body and spirit, I retired early to my bed and slept and slept. Though there were several prominent foreigners in the city to see me, among them Captain Wise, of the United States Navy, and though Baron Mollendorff [a confidential and business agent of the Viceroy's] left word that he had urgent matters to lay before me, I gave strict injunctions that I was to be disturbed on no consideration. As I say, I slept and slept; therefore to-day I feel at least half a dozen years younger, and shall undoubtedly be able to meet all callers in good humour.

"In the hour since the morning meal — which here in Tientsin all the Americans and English call 'tiffin,' while at home they call it by some other name — I have thought much of my friend Li Hsia Ying, who is now safely stored away in the fortress at Paoting-fu.

"I was compelled, indeed, to laugh at the old fellow who has been such a mischievous old devil at Seoul for years past, and who, in his own stone-hearted way, was hurrying us on to war with Japan. He is not the Tai Wen Kun, the Chief Court Lord, now; but a very meek and humble prisoner, who spends much of his time in wondering when his head will be severed from his body! I did not desire that the old man should suffer mentally, and, upon his first entrance to the Yamen, took occasion to tell him that no trouble whatever would befall him unless he were foolish enough to attempt to return to Seoul.

"'But I belong in Seoul, in Korea,' he exclaimed. 'Why was I put into a bag [kidnapped] and brought here to China?'

"I told him in plain language that he had been

a seriously disturbing element in Seoul, and that for that reason we had thought it best to remove him to a place where he could do no harm.

"'But I am of royal blood,' he exploded upon gaining his second breath, 'and neither Your Excellency nor any one else has the right to kidnap me!'

"In one way it was quite serious, and in another most laughable, and I could not help saying to the one-time Chief Court Lord that history was full of instances in which royal blood, when its owners were not careful, had the habit of running the wrong way. This appeared to quiet the old fellow, if not his fears, at least his voice, and he immediately began in whispers to ask what the Court intended doing with him.

"I have arranged that the former Chief Regent spend some time in the fortress of Paoting-fu, where he will be treated with every consideration due his former and present positions, and be kept out of mischief; for he is, indeed, a mischief-maker in a political way. We have just now enough to contend with in Korea; but a man can always watch his enemies, while he is never able to say what next folly his friends will accomplish. Thus it is with our good friend Li Hsia Ying. But he is safe now."

"*December* 19, 1882. — The Hong-Kong journals print an American despatch which says that the editors in the United States regard my removal of

the Tai Wen Kun from Seoul to China as a very
high-handed outrage; and these American papers
speak of Tai as being the great friend of the United
States, saying that it was he and he alone in all
Korea who exhibited enlightenment sufficient to
receive the American expedition in 1867.

"This is clearly a mistake, for the expedition of
1867 was not received in Korea at all, nor in all
likelihood would there to-day be a treaty between
the United States and Korea but for the writer of
these lines. Last year, about this time, Commodore Shufeldt, of the United States Navy, who
led the futile expedition of 1867, came to me here
in Tientsin. And in this very room we two discussed
and went over the subject of a new mission to Korea.
Between us we wrote the draft of the treaty that
was finally agreed upon at Seoul between the Tai
Wen Kun and Commodore Shufeldt.

"Furthermore, let it be noted for the benefit of
history that an escort of my own men accompanied
the American naval officer to Chemulpo, the entire
party being carried in a ship belonging to me personally, and Commander Shufeldt carrying from me
one of the strongest letters I have ever written. That
letter was directed to Li Hsia Ying, acting King of
Korea, who was urged — if he cared for the friendship of the Viceroy of Pechili — to bring his Government to the signing of the document carried by the
American naval officer. The treaty was signed; and
now the Americans, because I invite the Tai Wen

Kun to be the guest of China, call my action high-handed — because he was the Americans' friend!"

In the Viceroy's manuscript is reference to a further treaty, modelled upon the one he and Commodore Shufeldt had prepared, as having also been signed by the Tai Wen Kun and his ministers, and by [the document is here torn and the names obliterated] . . . on behalf of Great Britain.

"*Paoting-fu*, 1883. — To-day I had as my guest at two meals my old friend Li Hsia Ying. He is chafing under the mild restraint imposed upon him, and declares that if his life would be prolonged he must be allowed to return to Korea, in order, he says, that he may be with his family. When I told him that the Throne had decided that he must remain in China, at least for some months longer, he became at first excited and afterwards depressed, finally declaring that he would make away with himself if some change in his position were not brought about. I asked him if he desired more servants or less. And he replied excitedly: —

"'Less! Less! Take the whole damned lot away and I shall be happy.'

"Thus some men, even with every earthly need provided them, are not contented."

The Viceroy's diary does not contain any further reference to the enforced visit of the Chief Court

Lord of Korea, with the exception of a single brief entry, unaccompanied by a date, which simply remarks: "I hope His High Excellency Li Hsia Ying is now satisfied," leaving the searcher in doubt whether at the time of its making the old ex-king had, as he threatened, "made away" with himself, or had been allowed to return to his longed-for Seoul.

(Without date.) — "Affairs in Korea have come to such a pass that it is necessary at this juncture to announce fully our position, and I have sent to the Imperial Resident, for presentation to the Japanese Minister, and through him to the Government of Japan, a statement of Imperial claims with reference to the political status of that country. I have communicated the matter fully to Peking, and my action is already given hearty accord.

"The Japanese have no claims, inherited or acquired, in Chosen [Korea], and we deny the right of the Mikado's representative, or representatives, or subjects, to interfere with the internal workings of that vassal kingdom. Nor has any other Power whatsoever, outside China, the right to partake in the affairs of that country, internal or external. There can be no question of the absolute right of full suzerainty, if not of actual sovereignty, of the Throne [China] in Korea; and it is high time that the Japanese understood our unequivocal position in this regard.

"I have directed that my proclamation on behalf of the Throne be delivered to the King [of Korea], and that it be published upon the walls of the city [Seoul] and at other cities and ports of the tributary kingdom.

"It is a gauntlet thrown down to the pygmy and presumptuous Japanese; but the various foreign Governments represented at Seoul, including the Russian, the American, and the British, have asked for a definition of our position.

"From all my correspondence during five or six years, but more especially from personal interviews with the ministers and special representatives of the Powers within the past year, I am convinced that Japan s pretensions in Korea are viewed with great disfavour throughout the world; and I am confidently of the opinion that China has and will continue to have the moral support of the leading nations so far as her claims to suzerainty in Korea are concerned. Some of them may not fully acquiesce in our present partial claim to sovereignty, but none of them will give moral backing to Japan in any of her new-formed pretensions."

"*May*, 1883. — With the entire approval of the Treasury and the Council, and in full personal belief that it is the only correct course to pursue in the present unsatisfactory state of Korean finances, I have appointed Baron von Mollendorff head of the Customs Service, and he will proceed again to Seoul.

His several visits to the country, his able understanding of the language and the people, and, above all, his keen ability in the realm of finance, make him well suited to the place. I look for better results in every way, and am confident the King's financial affairs will shortly be at least upon a creditable basis.

"Mollendorff will also act for me as Foreign Adviser to the King, and thereby prevent any unwise moves on the part of His Majesty."

Baron von Mollendorff, who had long been in the confidence of Li Hung Chang, was, prior to his appointment as head of the Korean Customs, in the personal employ of the Viceroy. It appears from various entries in the latter's diary that he had great admiration for the business ability and integrity of the German, admitting him to an intimate knowledge of his own industrial and political affairs. As appears in the last entry, the Viceroy placed great hopes upon the Baron's expected accomplishments in Seoul; but subsequent notes in his journal, made in 1884 and 1885, tell mildly of his disappointment in Mollendorff's conduct, personal and official, while in the Korean capital; and finally of his vindictiveness against the German, when it was brought to the Viceroy's attention that during the former's term of service at Seoul he was secretly in correspondence with other Governments relative to the affairs of the Hermit Kingdom. It appears that Mollendorff, fearing his duplicity had been discovered, — which, in fact, was not the case, — quickly left Korea, taking with him an unknown amount of the public moneys.

In 1885 the Customs Service of the country was taken in charge by Sir Robert Hart, then and for many years the highly able and conscientious head of the Imperial Chinese Customs and Telegraphs.

CHAPTER XVIII

THE CESSION OF FORMOSA

IN one of the longest of his single political manuscripts, sufficiently lengthy in itself to make a fair-sized pamphlet, Viceroy Li deals with the cession of Formosa to the Japanese. He calls the island by its ancient Chinese name, Taiwan, but in a number of places refers to it variously as the "Land of Pirates," the "Island of Brown Robbers," etc. The monograph was written probably during the year 1897, for in it he refers to "my excuses to the Throne" (on the same subject). In the monograph he quotes from the last mentioned as "sent in the ninth moon of 1896": —

"It will some day be seen that I rendered my country a distinct service when I gave over Formosa [Taiwan] to the Japanese enemy. I do not expect that the country generally, or the world, will recognise this for many years to come, for political prejudices linger long in the minds of people, especially those most intimately concerned. We of to-day bless Ping Ti [an emperor reigning about the beginning of the Christian era] for his encouragement of sweet ballads and his cultivation of the graces. But, as Ha-Po tells us, there were thousands and thousands of people of his time who said that he was a Woman-

King, and should be rubbing oil upon the head of a
husband.

"From my earliest knowledge of things relating
to the whole country, I was most stoutly of the opinion that this Land of the Brown Robbers was a vile
spot, in which no man, even if he had the swiftest
of the running sicknesses [reference is made to
leprosy], would ever care to live. My father, after
one of his journeys to the sea, told me of having seen
many of the brown pirates brought to land and cut
in small pieces, and the pieces, he said, were scattered far apart in order that these fierce fellows
would never be able to grow together again.

"But while such tales impressed me in my younger
years, I did not let them influence my opinions when
I could study these matters from facts and reports
and common knowledge. I knew that while the
island, like Boko-To, the Pescadores, paid some
tribute to the Throne, and paid the tribute regularly
every seven moons, this was only to throw sand in
the eyes of the people so that the cut-throats might
better rob and plunder. It was as if one of my
servants would bring me a wild duck as a present,
making me think well of him, while his whole object
was to plunder my own fine fowl ponds.

"In after years I made considerable study of this
possession of the Throne which was the cause of so
much worry to all the Canton river-men, and even
up and down the coast from Macao to Shanghai.
More than that, by preying upon the vessels of

foreigners they were bringing the Viceroys and even the Government at the Northern Capital into wars and money troubles. Yet all this time they were paying tribute, and this tribute was being received with smiles and gladness.

"It may not be known generally, but as early as 1873, when complaints came to Tientsin from British traders, I earnestly memorialised the Throne to offer Taiwan to the English Government to do with the wretched island as they saw fit.

"It was the first memorial of the kind I had addressed to the Sacred Car, and it nearly cost me my position as well as my head. Being summoned to Peking, I was asked by the Grand Council what I meant by advocating that a part of the Imperial territory be given away; to which I replied that I was satisfied it was a hindrance rather than a benefit to the nation. If the great island could not be sold, I advocated that it be made a present to England. I told the Council that as England had been so ready to grab Hong-Kong we might in a measure get even with her by making a gift of Formosa. All manner of threats were made to me at the time of this visit, and I was requested to mind my most personal and provincial business. At that time I did not know that my words were striking so near the tribute-getters, but I learned afterward that while some of the same Grand Council agreed with me secretly as to the utter worthlessness of the possession, there were some reasons why they would not have the brown sea-rovers disturbed. I returned to Tientsin determined truly to be not too anxious regarding affairs outside my own sphere; and I believe that that one high reprimand was perhaps responsible for keeping me from more serious meddlings during the years when I still had not an army behind me, nor money in my chests, nor rice in my warehouses.

"A poor man is ever at a disadvantage in matters of public concern. When he rises to speak, or writes a letter to his superiors, they ask: Who is this fellow that offers advice? And when it is known that he is without coin they spit their hands at him, and use his letters in the cooks' fires. But if it be a man of wealth who would speak or write or denounce, even though he have the brain of a yearling dromedary, or a spine as crooked and unseemly, the whole city listens to his words and declares them wise.

"And just so it is with the man in office who is not yet possessed of sufficient bannermen or stored wealth to make him strong. He may obtain his office through his learning or ability, but he holds it always at the mercy of some one who is higher than himself.

"We all crave office of some kind, if that only of a village headman or an inspector of canals; but that man who is the holder of a small office is forever on his back [i.e., in hot water]. Of course we must all begin in the lower grades, and prove by ability and learning that we are worthy of the higher ones; but during my years of small tenure I was con-

stantly miserable at heart, and I am sure, even with
the wealth my father gave me, that had it not been
for the friendship of Tseng-kofan, and the chances
for advancement that came through the military
branch — which I once so despised — I should have
turned to agriculture and horticulture alone as my
life's work."

Tseng-kofan, of whom Li here speaks, was the
great Viceroy of Nanking, who gave the author his
first opportunity as a military leader, and to whom
extended references are made in other parts of the
memoirs.

"That former memorial made to the Throne was
cast into my face when I returned from the peace
negotiations with Japan, and for one reason I was
glad that it was; for it entirely disproved the words
of the carpers, who were maintaining, on the one
hand, that our enemies had bribed me into turning
Formosa over to them, and, on the other hand, that
I was browbeaten by the Japanese, and had no
bravery of heart nor strength of mind.

"Last year, in the ninth moon, in writing my
free and full excuses to Their Majesties, I wrote in
part as follows regarding the cession of Formosa:
'The records of the Grand Council will show, I
believe — if they are as truthfully kept and preserved
as it is important they should be — that as much as
twenty-three years ago I memorialised the Throne,

or at least attempted to, to the effect that Taiwan was a black ulcer spot upon the beautiful and sacred body of the empire, and that to cause its removal, by whatever means, would be a blessing to the country. It cannot be said that at that time I was in any league with our enemies the Japanese. My heart was as full of hatred for them at one time as at another, and no one—excepting my own countrymen—can accuse me of a fondness for Nippon, the Japanese least of all. In 1873 I nearly lost my office because I would advocate the giving away of a worse than worthless possession, and now I am accused of a weakness of spirit because at Shimonoseki I agreed to give them something that I was certain China did not want.'

"It is true that when Marquis Ito stipulated, as one of the chief terms of peace, that Formosa should be ceded, I immediately declared that I was willing to agree to almost anything but that; yet, had I been in another apartment, all alone, I should have danced for joy in spite of all my infirmities. As it was my heart was indeed glad, but I requested the chief plenipotentiary to say at least that the Mikado would not insist upon having the big island. His Excellency agreed to put the question over until the next session of the commissioners, and during the intervening time I was sore afraid he would change his mind and announce that his Government did not want it. On the contrary, however, upon the reassembling of the negotiators, the Japanese members insisted that Formosa be ceded to the Mikado, and, after much parley, I reluctantly agreed. All the members of our party fully agreed with me that we were doing particularly well in getting rid of the possession, and it was my expectation that the Throne and the Ministers would also look upon the matter in the same light.

"But I have found that you cannot hope always, even when you are doing your best, for the approbation of others. More times than many during the past two years have I heard it said in high quarters that I traded away a most valuable possession, yet I will tell my countrymen, that they may know it now and remember it in the future, that at that peace conference I should almost have been willing to add Formosa to any demands the Mikado should make — if those demands could have been agreed to at all — and to pay him something additional for taking the island off our hands.

"What could China want of such an ulcer possession? In the first instance, had Formosa been of any real value, England or France would have made pretensions to it years ago, and we should have lost it by force of arms, just as we have lost other territory along that coast. But these Westerners knew its real value, — or its real worthlessness, I should say, — and the island was left in our undisturbed possession. If we were a naval power, as years ago I urged we should be, declaring myself ready to spend millions of taels of my own money in the building of a Chinese navy that would give us some real strength at sea, we might find some little use for Formosa as a naval base; but as a colony, a possession, or a province, it was a distinct injury to China from the first day it owned allegiance to the Throne.

"It is not as if the Formosans were really people of the Mongolian race. They are neither of us nor with us, and we praise all the ancestors that this is so! In all Asia, in all the world, I believe, there are no tribes of animals called men more degraded and filthy than these people of Taiwan. And have we not enough of criminals and low creatures to deal with on the mainland? These people are not farmers, they are not hill-men, nor hunters of wild beasts whose skins bring in money and keep men's bodies warm in the cold winters. No, they are not even fit to be soldiers in trained armies, for they have no discipline, nor could they be taught. Neither would they make good sailors on regular ships, though many of the coastmen are good enough as wild pirates and buccaneers of the sea. They are cut-throats, all of them, along the coasts and back in the jungles. And so they have been from the days of Chia-Ch'ing to the present time.

"No, they are not all even of so good a class as that! For what are opium-smokers, head-hunters, and filthy lepers? I know from all I have learned in official and commercial quarters — the latter

when I was President of the North Sea Trade —
that a very large number of these people are opium-
users of the lowest kind, and those who do not use
the hellish concoction only abstain from it because
it is not within their power or means to obtain that
dirtiest of evil drugs, which England has for fifty
years forced upon the people of China. If the opium
could not be obtained from the near-by coast ports,
if our own merchant seamen were not compelled to
carry the vile stuff, neither could the islanders of
Formosa have obtained it and made themselves so
low in the moral scale.

"I am perfectly well aware that some of our statesmen have expressed great expectations regarding the
future of the island; and by some the building of the
Tainan railway-line was regarded as the beginning
of real industrial and financial progress. But I myself talked several times with Lin Ming Ching about
that railroad enterprise, as well as other proposed
industrial undertakings, and Ching — who had formerly been an enthusiast — declared finally that
he had lost faith in the island as a place of investment. This was in strange contrast with his language of former years, when he came to me and
proposed that I furnish capital for some mining
projects in the interior. As a matter of fact I had,
and still have, small amounts invested in properties in
Takow and Tainan; but I shall look for no greater
returns from them than I believe Japan will receive
from her political investment.

"If China did not have hundreds of millions of acres in the west, millions of them in Mongolia, millions in Kiangsu and Shensi, untold millions even in the far western provinces and in Tibet, that are as yet unpeopled, we might be drawn to this great island and attempt its regeneration. But with these vast areas unpeopled and untilled, what do we want of the wild forests of Formosa, filled as they are with head-hunters and opium-eaters?

"The island is unsavoury in history, even from the time of Chia-Ch'ing and beyond; and great outlays of money and means have been necessary at various times to put down millions of these vile robbers. Think of the great Kashgaria outbreak and what it cost! And in the good Chien Lung's reign many lives and much treasure were exhausted in quelling the wild rebellions that broke forth. Can any one name a single man born in Formosa who has brought either glory or treasure to China? Some will answer, 'Yes, Koxinga'; and perhaps I will agree, for Koxinga did do one good thing, — at least good for the Dutch, — he drove them from the island!

"It will be said by those who are my enemies — and perhaps not denied by my friends — that this paper is written wholly with the idea of defending my personal name in this matter. In a sense, of course, this is true; but in a very much larger sense it is not true, for the principal object of this writing is to convince my countrymen that in the ceding of Formosa to the Japanese, China has really not lost anything of value; instead, she will eventually be the gainer thereby. We never have been in a position to defend the possession, were it worth defending, from any Western Power, nor even from Japan in later years. And in all times of necessity must it have been a menace to our international relations. England, entrenched forever at Hong-Kong, would have been no stronger in possession of Formosa; yet for the balance of power in Eastern waters I should much prefer to see the island in possession of the Japanese. They, in course of time, may find some use for it in their sea operations, or as a dumping-ground for millions of their coolies, who, otherwise, must eventually overrun Korea and the mainland. But I am sure that in the years to come they will not regard me in the light of such a noble giver as some of my critics would have China to-day believe."

CHAPTER XIX

ESTIMATES OF PROMINENT PERSONS

THE CZAR OF RUSSIA

(WRITTEN at Peking in August, 1897.) — "The mails brought me a handsome new portrait of the Czar and Czarina of Russia to-day, richly framed and accompanied by a long personal note from His Majesty. It is already hanging in my own room beside those other portraits which Their Majesties were pleased to present to me during my visit to Moscow.

"I shall never cease to think most happily of the Czar, nor forget the very great consideration he showed me in Russia. There were, of course, many vital questions regarding Eastern affairs upon which he desired to obtain my views; and I was quite as anxious to learn what were his intents and purposes with reference to matters of great interest and import to China. But, aside from all political considerations, His Majesty treated me quite as a visiting sovereign at St. Petersburg and Moscow rather than as a mere Special Ambassador to his coronation. The good Czarina, too, — I could tell by her face that she was a good woman as well as a good Empress, — treated me with a consideration that is pleasing to a man of my years.

"I am not sure whether it was five or six audiences I had with the Czar during my stay. I use the word 'audiences,' but they were not that. Only one or two were of the formal or ceremonial kind, and at these other envoys were present. But the others were simply face to face visits, with good tea, good wine, and, I suppose the Europeans would call it, good music.

"Of course, it gave me great pleasure to thank the Czar for having especially requested the Throne that I be sent as China's representative to the coronation. Another, whom I need not now name, had been chosen to represent the Sacred Car [Their Chinese Majesties] at the great ceremonies; but almost at the last hour Nicholas himself sent word by telegraph that my appointment would be most pleasing to him. There was nothing then for the Palace, especially in view of our recent negotiations with the Russian Government, but to send me instead. I had never intended to leave China, that is, as a mere sight-seer about the globe; but the Czar's request gave me good opportunity for viewing some of the other great countries of the world, especially Russia, Germany, France, Belgium, and England in Europe, and the great United States in America.

"During one of my evening visits to the Czar the conversation was almost wholly upon the trip he had taken to the Far East when Crown Prince of Russia. During that journey he had learned quite a number of Chinese phrases, some of them quite long and involved; and these he repeated to me at intervals during the evening. He referred laughingly to the attempt that had been made on his life by one of my own countrymen; and remarked that now, after being a Czar, he was getting accustomed to such things. At this remark the whole company — there were perhaps a dozen persons in the room — laughed; all with the exception of Count Witte and myself, for I see no humour in assassination.

"During all my personal visits to His Majesty he was as a very approachable and democratic man, although I knew, of course, that not many of [his subjects could get as near to him as I had. Yet his manner was free and unrestrained, though he was ordinarily most quiet if not actually modest or 'backward.' At first I was very ill at ease in his presence, but when he offered first cigars, then cigarettes, with his own hands, and touched glasses over fine wines, I felt that I was simply the guest of a Russian gentleman, and not an envoy to the great Czar of the most extensive empire of the world.

"Before leaving St. Petersburg His Majesty loaded me with many personal gifts — for the Dowager Empress and the Emperor, the ladies of the Forbidden City, and for Lady Li and myself. Among those for myself was a rich robe of sable, lined with purple satin, which I am told is worth at least 15,000 taels. This I shall wear only when the most auspicious occasions fall upon the coldest days."

SIR ROBERT HART

(Without date.) — "The entire finances of the Customs have been placed in the hands of a foreigner, Sir Robert Hart, and it is predicted there will not hereafter be a stringency in official circles. Let us hope that it may be so, although I am firmly convinced that we have native bankers, among them [here many Chinese names are given] . . . who could as well administer the office. Sir Robert is highly commended by the British Government; a very natural thing since the Britishers are always worrying lest they lose a few pounds in their Oriental investments."

"1883. — It has been suggested that I turn over the Korean finances to the administration of Sir Robert Hart, but I am not quite prepared to do this. Personally I have large sums at stake in connection with Korean affairs, and I should prefer to obtain my own before trusting all to this administrator, whose methods are sometimes to be questioned."

"*December*, 1890. — Perhaps of all the foreigners who have taken service under the Government there is no man of as clean and honourable record as Sir Robert Hart, who was my visitor and dinner-guest yesterday. In the first years of our acquaintance, nearly a quarter of a century ago, I was inclined to distrust him — but I distrust all men until I know them; yet as I have come to know him better, and to study from year to year what he has accomplished, I do not hesitate to say that in this Irish-Britisher the empire has found one of its truest and most loyal friends, as well as an administrator of finances who is as honest and painstaking as he is brilliant and pleasing."

MR. GLADSTONE

"As I wrote during my world journey, if I could not be Li Hung Chang I should next prefer to be the Prime Minister of England. It is true I should not want to have his ailments, and I presume he would not like to possess my rheumatism and heart troubles; but Mr. Gladstone made a deep impression upon me during the few hours I was at his home. He appeared to me as a man not only of great mentality but of wonderful strength of will and courage of conviction. His face looked to me more honest than any other I had seen in all Europe, and I believe if such a man as he were at the head of England's affairs no great wrong would ever be done by that Government."

GOVERNOR HASTINGS OF PENNSYLVANIA

"They tell me that Napoleon was a very small man, who did not at all look like an emperor. When I saw General Hastings, in Philadelphia, it occurred to me that Napoleon, with all his armies and territories, should have looked like this gallant American!

"I have heard that he is since dead, but I hope that it is not so, for I had intended writing him upon my return to China, and I also very much wished to send him enough of the finest tea to last his family all their days.

"Though he looked so like what an emperor ought to look, or as a fine general-in-chief of a tremendous victorious army, General Hastings was indeed a warm-hearted, jovial man, with pure humour all over his handsome face. We sat together for some hours in a semi-official hotel or club in Philadelphia, and it was most unfortunate that we could not converse in a common language without the use of interpreters. These latter are most annoying to me when social matters are under discussion. They spoil one's remarks, and oftentimes do not understand the point themselves. In political or business life they may be tolerated; in fact, they are sometimes very useful as witnesses."

PRESIDENT CLEVELAND

"It was a source of regret to me that I could not get from President Cleveland a promise to visit the Far East as his illustrious predecessor General Grant — who put down the American rebellion during those years when I was ridding China of the Taipings — had done seventeen years before. If Mr. Cleveland had said he would make a visit to China it would have been my great honour and pleasure to arrange for him the most elaborate and distinguished reception ever accorded a great man in China. But the American President would not give me the faintest hope in this respect, declaring that when his days of office were finished he hoped to go to some quiet place in the country, and no more take an active part in the public affairs of the United States.

"'There will be younger, better, and abler men to look after the country's well-being,' he said.

"It was and still is difficult for me to understand this attitude, for, after all his years of power at the head of a great people, I could not see how he should want to relinquish so much and go voluntarily into private life. It is not the way with us here in China.

"I asked the President what his age was, and he told me, but I have forgotten just the number of years. I believe they were as many as fourteen or fifteen less than my own. He said that he had no infirmity of moment, and that he enjoyed the woods and the fields, boating, hunting, and fishing. (How the people of China would stare if they should see the Emperor, or even myself, fishing!) Mr. Cleveland looked to me like one who had spent much of his life outdoors; a strong, heavy man, who reminded me much of Bismarck, except that his face was not so florid, nor his voice so loud."

SIR NICHOLAS O'CONOR

"In all my dealings with this fine British Minister I have found him above the slightest reproach.

During his time in Korea I was in close touch with all his movements, and it was with great pleasure that I heard of his transfer to Peking. After he came here we became warm personal friends; but that did not at any time interfere with the battles we were almost constantly, for a number of years, compelled to wage."

MARQUIS ITO

"He was always a hard man to make a bargain with, but this perversity and stubbornness was not personal. It belongs to the nation of which he was so distinguished a representative. Kind at heart, and a gentleman by nature, he was forever driven by those behind him at Tokio to present a front of almost unrelenting severity. He served his country well — much better than she deserved."

UNITED STATES MINISTER CONGER

"I have come to know His Excellency Major Conger, of the United States Legation, as I have known few Americans; and Madam Conger and Lady Li are well known to each other. Major Conger was here [Peking residence] yesterday, and together we went over the events of the late [Boxer] outbreak; not as opposing diplomats endeavouring to learn secrets from each other, but as friends who have seen one of the most dangerous incidents in all Chinese history lose its terrible importance and be smoothed over. Minister Conger, backed by the

United States, was a strong friend of my country's during those fearful weeks. I tremble to think of what might have been China's fate but for the stand taken by the American Government."

CHAPTER XX

THE OPIUM HABIT AND TRAFFIC

If the expression is permissible, the diary of Viceroy Li is as thickly dotted with references to the opium habit and traffic as are the poppy-fields with the bloom of the drug-giving plant in the June days. He appears to have been a violent hater of the devastating narcotic and its votaries from youth to old age, yet he frankly tells of his own engagement in opium culture, "for the sake of medicine and medicine alone," and does not hesitate to say that some parts of his estates in Hupeh were "leased for its culture." Altogether, those parts of his diary and memoirs relating to the subject, especially in view of the heroically drastic measures adopted by the Chinese Republic for the suppression of the use of and traffic in opium, are without doubt among the most interesting of all his writings.

The earliest reference found in his diary proper appears to have been written in 1845, when he was still a student at Hofei, about, indeed, the time of the so-called Opium War. It follows.

"It is not only for weeks but for many months that I have laboured with my good friend Ho-Kai to prevail upon him to abstain from the vice which has found its way into the neighbourhood; but with the quitting of his interest in all things I fear my

words and counsel have been wasted. Yet I blame
his father more than any one else, for the old swine-
raiser brought the habit into the family, and all his
sons make use of the terrible extract.

"To-day I sought out Ho-Kai in his home, but his
mother told me he was seldom there now, for he
spends much of his time in the walled village in
drunken stupor. His father does likewise, and at
least one of his brothers. It would seem as if, when
the scourge attacks one of a family, it does not spare
many of its members, and that in the second generation its hold is worse than in the first. Oh, how
thankful I am that Heaven has spared our family,
that my father taught us to avoid this evil! Why will
a man like Ho-Kai, senior, bring corruption directly
to his own home? Does it not show how low the
victim of this vice will fall?

"This day, though my father has warned me
strictly to avoid his company, I went into the high
village in search of Ho-Kai. It was no trouble to find
him, for the vile place where he spends most of his
time is now known to all the neighbourhood, since
it is said that more than two hundred in this district
are users of the foreign drug. My friend, whom I
met outside the place on his way home, grew angry
with me when I protested at his unseemly conduct.
But I was willing to stand his anger for his sister's
sake, and for his mother's, for the family is of the
shan-sz [the local gentry], and we have ever been
on most intimate terms with them. Besides, a

good aunt of Ho-Kai's is a secondary wife of my father's, and a much-respected woman. Yet my former friend and schoolmate would not listen to my words, declaring that he now loves the foreign drug more than he ever did the classics. Is it not wonderful how a good man, though not greatly talented, will put his head into the fu-nun, the tiger's mouth?"

"*Later* [without date]. — Ho-Kai's father is dead; it is the foreign drug which killed him, though some believe that he took too much, knowing that the respect in which his former associates held him was forever gone, and his property in the hands of the usurers. Ho-Kai, himself, is no longer at his home, but one of the miserable beggars of the highway. His eyes are nearly blind, though he is some years younger than myself. When I went along the road yesterday he did not know me. I should be glad to see him die, too; and I believe it will not be long before he follows his father."

A dozen years later, when Li Hung Chang was the commander of the victorious Imperial troops at Nanking, he wrote: —

"We found the great city full of the opium evil, and hundreds who had not had solid food for many days were still sufficiently supplied with this terrible curse, so that they slept and dreamed through the riot and battle about them. To General Ching I gave orders that all persons found with the drug in their possession, all persons under its baneful influence, and all persons, of whatever force they had been or were allied to, who sought the drug either for their own use or to engage in the profitable business of trafficking in it, should be decapitated.

"Immediately upon receiving these orders, General Ching was indiscreet enough to enter into argument with General Gordon, though I have forbidden the former to arouse the Englishman. After I had severely reprimanded him he went upon the errand assigned him, and this morning reported that he had executed more than twelve hundred users and retailers of the drug. It is good work, and it further commends Ching in my sight.

"Once, without intending in the least to hurt the English gentleman's feelings, I spoke of his countrymen as being largely to blame for the importation of opium into the land. The occasion for the remark was the giving of the order by myself for the death by ling-chi [cutting to bits] of an officer of the Shantung bannermen, who had sold the drug among the officers of our force, but who himself neither smoked nor ate it.

"General Gordon flew into a terrible fit of anger without waiting for me to explain that I but uttered the words in jest so far as he was personally concerned, and declared that he should not be surprised if it were true that a few low Englishmen could be found willing to engage in the trade; but, he added, there were millions of low Chinese ready for it when it was brought to them. I did not like his remark, and told him so; but the subject was not spoken of again between us, for he was quite as great an opium hater as myself. It was because of my knowing this, as well as of his very sensitive national pride, that I had warned Ching.

"Viceroy Tseng-kofan used the drug somewhat during his younger days, though not to excess. His mind is wonderfully strong, and it is not difficult for me to believe that even with great temptations about him he would not fall victim to this abuse as easily as other men. If I remember rightly, he once told me that for a while, during his younger scholastic days, he felt that the foreign curse was getting the better of him, and that his great devotion to mathematics saved him from ruin. Yes, I am sure it was Tseng-kofan, but whether he told me directly, or I heard it concerning him, I cannot now remember. However, he knew that his power of solving problems of astronomy and mathematics was leaving him, and he determined forever to abandon the drug."

" *Viceregal Yamen, Tientsin*, 1893. — A statement has been translated to me from one of the London papers, in which I am quoted as saying to the Honourable George N. Curzon that I do not, in common with most Chinese, hold Great Britain responsible for the importation of opium into China.

"In the first place, I never in my life made such

an outrageous assertion; in the second place, I feel
sure that Mr. Curzon never said I did; and, in the
third place, both Mr. Curzon and myself, as well as
every well-read and intelligent Britisher or Oriental,
is aware of the unhappy and disgraceful fact that
but for Great Britain there would not be a picul of
opium sold in China to-day for illegitimate use; by
this I mean for use outside the legitimate practice
of medicine.

"This may appear to be a strong assertion, and I
have no doubt it will be as strongly denied and condemned; but it is a true one, nevertheless, and the
entire history of trade and traffic in the Orient will
substantiate my every word.

"A great many fine Englishmen have been friends
of mine, and I number to-day many of that race
among my intimates: ministers and consuls, army
and navy officers, engineers, and hundreds and hundreds of merchants. These men know that I have
great admiration for them and their race, and, in all
seasons and times, for their sacred and virtuous
Queen. But for the Government, so far as it has
made itself not only the agent but the guardian of
the vicious opium trade, I have a very sincere dislike.

"I know that, because of this money-grasping,
trade-compelling feature of England's dealings with
my country, millions of wretched people of China
have been made more miserable; stalwart men and
women have been made paupers, vagrants, and the
lowest of criminals; and hundreds of thousands of

the weaker ones of my race — mainly among the women — have been sent to suicide graves.

"And all this because otherwise India might not prosper!

"And all this because otherwise British trade might not flourish in Chinese ports!

"All this because gold and territory are greater in the eyes of the British Government than the rights and bodies of a weak people.

"Yes! Yes! Yes! We Chinese have been laughed and sneered at in the streets of London itself, and have been called 'Pig-tailed Opium-Eaters,' when for years and years it is the Government of these same Londoners which has been responsible for the millions of human wrecks throughout the length and breadth of the Middle Kingdom.

"I was asked once by a British admiral at Amoy what my estimate of the number of opium-users in China would be. I did not reply directly, but questioned him as to the population of England; and when he told me in the neighbourhood of 27,000,000, I said: 'Admiral, that is about the number of opium fiends in China.'

"He said he did not get my meaning.

"Then I told him that, as his country was responsible for the vicious traffic, each man and woman and child in England might well feel that there was at least one wretched being in China as a representative.

"In this relation I have often taken my pen and

from records before me made estimates of the number of unfortunates in this great empire of ours; and each time have my figures told me that about one tenth of our people are victims of a vice that has no parallel anywhere on earth. I could wish that I might make the figure smaller, but as I have gone over my calculations time and time again, and as they include the most wretchedly diseased provinces of Yunnan and Szechuan, I feel that my estimates are too low rather than too high.

"It must not be imagined that I am so ignorant of history as to claim that England or any other of the Western nations was responsible for the introduction of the cursed drug into China. No, it came from the island of Java two hundred years before the 'Opium War,' gaining its strongest hold along the coast and in Formosa. Kang H'sai sent an official to enquire into the evil in Formosa, and he died there. Others followed, became addicted to the curse, and died also. Later, travellers and traders, crossing from India and the Mohammedan countries, introduced it into the western provinces; and, still later, this devil's extract entered the country as gifts to princes and others in high places.

"I am fully aware of the growth of the vice in China, for even as a boy at school I saw its ravages, and I enquired whence it came, and why it was brought. Even a bosom friend and student — whose name I do not just now recall — became a victim of the habit, left his home, and was finally stoned to death by order of the magistrate because he had become entirely bereft of reason and decency.

"Yes, in all my years — in my studies, in the army, during the wars and the famines, in all my political and business life, I have studied and combated this devouring evil; and the more I know and see and learn of it the greater does England's crime become in my eyes. England — proud and mighty and rich England — England with her great armies and navies and great men — is shamed and covered with ignominy because of the crimes of her Indian poppy!

"It has been stated times without number, and upon several occasions directly to my face, that while I was seemingly opposed to the traffic, I myself, personally or through agents, had dealt in the drug, having grown poppy upon my own lands, and having leased lands both in Hupeh and Pechili for its cultivation. I have never denied the truth of these statements, and in this writing (a copy of which I intend to send to the 'Times' correspondent at Peking and another to the Honourable Mr. Curzon) I shall acknowledge that the foregoing assertions are true.

"But I will immediately say, in order that my honour and my conscience be satisfied, that to my knowledge not one farthing's worth of the opium in which I dealt ever went for smoking purposes. I would have my secretary prepare, if such were necessary, a list of the high medical firms and men with whom I have had business dealings in opium, and it could easily be shown that they are not only of the best medical repute in China, Japan, and Russia, but that they, almost without exception, — I speak particularly of Chinese doctors and concerns where I have had dealings, — are as bitterly opposed to the habit and traffic as I myself am, such men and firms as could not be approached by users of the drug, or by users' agents in any way. Of course, so far as concerns what has become of the commodity sent to Japan and Russia, I cannot say; only I feel certain from the price and the grade dealt in that very little if any has ever reached the so-called drug fiend. As to the lands I have leased for agricultural purposes I can only say that never has there been a stipulation for or against the poppy; but where I have found the plant growing upon my lands I have always endeavoured as a mere matter of business to have the crude product sold to myself.

"And still another view of this question has been taken. The Chinese Government has, on more than a few occasions, been asked almost directly this question: 'If you regard the importation of opium into your country in the light of such a dire evil, why is it that you do not make and enforce laws prohibiting the growth of the poppy within your territory?' And our Government has always replied: 'Of what avail would it be when we are still "*compelled*" to open our ports to the drug from India?'

"Could any question, really a question from one Government to another, be more ridiculous and could any answer be more to the point?

"I know that for more than twenty years there have been repeated attempts made by outside interested parties to have the sternest edicts issued from the Northern Capital against the growth of the poppy throughout China. Mark me, not against the use of the drug, the deadly and benumbing drug, but against the cultivation of the plant from whose pod the poison is extracted!

"I know, furthermore, that large sums of money were ready to fall into the hands of certain high officials if they could secure such an edict from the Palace.

"What would the object of this be?

"The man who could not grasp the meaning of this knavish attempt would, indeed, lack the mentality of a blind toad!

"No; the rich Indians, backed by the diplomatic force and physical strength of the British Empire, would not alone rob millions of degraded Chinese of their mental and bodily strength, but they would sap the last cash from the land of their victims. They would drain our beloved country in every way, and leave us helpless dupes of the poppy farmers of India.

"I want to say that I am not of those of my countrymen who have been in opposition, either openly or secretly, to the advance of the Western

Church in China. On the contrary, I have from very early days welcomed the missionary of the West as well as the merchant or the engineer, and I hope to continue in this attitude to the end of my days; for it is my earnest belief that the sooner China awakens her vast body to all that is good in the West, without sacrificing her own virtues and high qualities, without neglecting her own splendid philosophy and beautiful literature, — the gifts of her sages and poets for centuries and centuries, — the sooner will she take her place among the Powers of this age, and the sooner will her people rise to a higher and better plane.

"But it must be understood by all the Western peoples that Christianity has suffered a much slower growth among the Chinese because of this one curse of opium. Indeed, what are our people, mandarin and coolie, rich man and pauper, scholar and unlettered man, to think, when they all know that the blackest and most deadly virus that has been injected into the nation, year after year, decade after decade, has been forced upon it by a Christian Power? It is not the scholarly and high and powerful who become converts to the Church of the West. No. Neither do these classes as a rule go into the gutters and to the prisons on account of the opium curse; but they see the vice all about them: the grovelling wrecks, the opiated bodies in the execution places, the wretched criminals, the deserted wives of the victims, and the unburied suicides upon the plains and along the paths. And they know that a great nation, a Christian nation above all things, has given this awful blight to the Middle Kingdom.

"What are they to think?"

THE END

APPENDIX

LI HUNG CHANG'S POETICAL WRITINGS ON OPIUM

ODE TO THE POPPY

(Date of writing unknown)

WHO would think to look upon you,
　　Nodding sweetly in the fields,
That the scented heart within you
　　Our soul's vilest passion yields?

Who would think to see your verdure,
　　In the Springtime lovely green,
That the garment nature gives you
　　Clothes such wickedness and spleen?

Who would think to note your sprouting
　　As a nurtured, tender child,
That the blood that ran within you
　　Carried visions fiendish wild?

Who would think to see your bowing
　　To the soothing winds of Spring,
That you sheltered in your bosom
　　Every bitterness and sting?

Who would think to see you pluming,
　　Like the peacock vain and proud,
That beneath your gorgeous feathers
　　Is a note discordant, loud?

Who would think that in the June-time,
　　When in myriads o'er the plain
You do look your brightest, sweetest,
　　That your smile was hidden pain?

Who would think that we who plant you,
    And who love to watch you grow,
Hate you, curse you, trample on you,
    When you bring us heart-deep woe?

Who would think that tender flower,
    Watched by children of the land,
Should return the fond love given
    By a stroke of foulest hand?

Who would think that in our garden,
    Where our eyes may ever see,
In disguise would grow a hell-weed,
    Deadly in its misery?

Who would think that in our day-dreams
    Of a home all undefiled
We should rear — O heaven spare us! —
    Such, in truth, a demon child?

THE SHAME OF GREAT ENGLAND

(*Written in* 1881)

GREAT England says she rules the widest sea
In might and right and white man's liberty.
Her armoured ships and regiments of war
Span seas and lands 'neath many skies afar.
She sends her learned sons (in Western ways well-taught),
Where'er her flag has been, her sons have fought;
And vast the good these Church and school men do —
If all Great England claims for them is true.

But has Great England in her lordly boast
Surveyed her pirate traders on our coast?
Or has she, while aloft her pride has tossed,
Vouchsafed one thought to what her fame has cost?
Her traders, sailing here from India's strand
In quest of gold and measures great of land,
Have brought within their greedy hands no good, —
But vessels large for China's ebbing blood!

Shame! shame! upon Great England of the West,
Upon her bristling guns and all the rest,
For know we not that in this grand array
Is sceptre grim to lure our souls away?
Not as a friend comes England to our shore,
But with a cry for blood and gold, and more:
The lives of countless thousands, steepèd deep
In her vile drug, in shameful homage creep.

TO ALL WHO WILL LISTEN

(An early composition)

To all who will listen I would warning give
Against the vile poppy juice.
But if you will not heed
Upon your own heads will fall calamity;
For in all the Middle Kingdom,
Even from the Yellow on the North
To the Pearl on the South,
And along the banks of the Great River
Back to the granite mountains of the West,
There is no evil such as this.

In the fields we see the poppy growing,
And the great fields are sights of gladness,
For the eye is pleased with the flowers,
And the scent is sweet to the nostrils,
And the birds are happy in their homes,
And the ground mice sport and play.
All is so innocent and good,
That we think of the rice and the maize,
And the orchard and the grasslands,
And they do not surpass the poppy.

Yes, and it would be so
If only we might let the flowers
Bloom and die to grow another year.
But men will not let it be so,
For from the flower the poison is drawn
And given to men to take away their minds.

O my brothers and all my friends,
If you would hearken to good advice,
Avoid the poppy juice forever and aye,
For it is a plague most noxious and vile!
It will eat out your minds,
It will rot away your vitals,
It will shrivel up your bowels,   ·
It will make you walk as a leper,
It will cast you into prison,
It will send you to your death!

But not only you, my friend, will be cast down!
No, look about you with clear eyes to-day:
See the misery and ruin it has wrought;
See the human wrecks on every side,
Lower than the swine of the far fields;
See the women bereft of home and all,
Now toiling in the hot sun of the day,
Each day of the long, long year,
That they may buy rice for their babies,
And give food to their own bodies!
Think of the graves of every village,
The graves you cannot see for want of care!
Do some care lightly for the palsied,
Or those whose veins do hold the plague?
Yes, in all hearts there is pity
For all that suffer other ills.
But for the user of the vilesome juice,
The smoker of the demon's pipe,
There is no pity in any heart,
No welcome in e'en the lowest home;
There is no shame too great for him,
No suffering he must not bear alone,
No depths too deep for him to sink into.
He thinks he lives in some sweet heaven,
Yet wakes to find that fearsome hell
Has been his own abode
And e'er will be.

𝕮𝖍𝖊 𝕽𝖎𝖛𝖊𝖗𝖘𝖎𝖉𝖊 𝕻𝖗𝖊𝖘𝖘

CAMBRIDGE . MASSACHUSETTS

U . S . A